# The Potawatomi Indians

*The History, Trails and Chiefs of the Potawatomi Native American Tribe*

By Otho Winger

Adansonia
Press

Logo art adapted from work by Bernard Gagnon

ISBN-13: 978-0-359-74751-1

First published in 1939

## CHIEF LEOPOLD POKAGON

*The Last Great Chief of the Potawatomi*

## TO JOE AND LOU ANN

*Who live on Nottawa Road*
*And may some day ask*
*What Nottawa means*

# Contents

# Preface

This book is one of the results of years of interest in, and study of, the American Indian. Former studies put in book form have been received with such favor that I have been encouraged to put out another volume. Former books have been about the Miami Indians. They were neighbors to the Potawatomi Indians and had much history in common. In the territory in which I do much work and travel, there are many places with Potawatomi names. Almost every county is rich in history and tradition about the red men who lived here but little more than a century ago. Much of this history and tradition is unknown to the present generation. To me it is not only interesting history but important as well.

At the close of the book is a bibliography of the main works I have read and from which I have gathered information. I am unable to list all the papers and books from which I have received impressions and information. I have visited most of the county libraries in this region and have read their pioneer histories and papers. I have received much help in the Indiana State Library and in the various libraries of Chicago. I have talked with many people both Indians and white men about these subjects. To all of these I owe my thanks. I owe special thanks to Alice M. Doner, Gletha Mae Noffsinger and Irene Winger for their help in preparing the manuscript; also to Inez Gochenour, Eugene Butler and Lorrell Eikenberry, for the maps and illustrations.

This book is sent forth with the hope that it will increase interest in local history and in the story of the Indians who preceded us and on whose lands we now live.

# Chapter One - The Potawatomi Indians and Their Early History

The Pot-a-wat-o-mi Indians were a tribe of the great Algonquin race, whose tribes stretched from the Atlantic to the Mississippi and beyond. The Potawatomi and the Ottawa were closely related to the Chippewa who were the Ojibway of Longfellow's Hiawatha. The three were probably one tribe in ancient days when, according to the legend of Longfellow, Hiawatha was their national hero.

Just when the Potawatomi left the parent family and become a separate tribe is not known. The usual explanation of the meaning of their name is "people of the place of fire." They were often spoken of as "fire builders" with various explanations as to how this name applied to them. Perhaps the most likely explanation is that when this group decided to become a tribe, separate from the parent family, they decided to build a council fire for themselves. So the name was suggested from "puttawa," blowing a fire, and "mi," a nation; that is, a people able to build their own national fire and exercise the right of self-government. The council fire was a very important thing in the life of a tribe, for it was the center of their national decisions. Some say that the Potawatomi were jealous of their national council fire, and never allowed it to go out. If so, the name "Put-ta-wa-mi" is significant. The name has been variously spelled, but the most prominent authorities in recent years have used the more simple form, Pot-a-wat-o-mi, with the accent on the first and third syllables.

The original home of the Potawatomi was with or near, the parent tribe in the great lake region of northern Michigan, on the western shores of Lake Huron. From here they were driven west by the powerful Iroquois. They were met by early European explorers on the western shore of Lake Michigan, near Green Bay, Wisconsin. Again they were found at Sault Ste. Marie, in the peninsula of northern Michigan, where they were fleeing from the powerful Sioux who came from the west. The Potawatomi, like some other Algonquin tribes, were found in various places, where they were trying to escape the vengeance of one or the other of these two great tribes.

The Potawatomi themselves became known as of two divisions. Those who moved south from the forests of northern Wisconsin into the prairies of northern Illinois and western Indiana became known as Prairie Potawatomi, or Mascoutens. Those who remained in the forests of northern Wisconsin and Michigan became known as the Potawatomi of the Woods, or Forest Potawatomi. In language, traditions, and customs, the Forest Potawatomi retained a closer relationship with the Chippewa and Ottawa. The Prairie

Potawatomi became the more important group and with them the early white men had important relationships.

By the close of the seventeenth century the Potawatomi had moved south from their northern homes into the Illinois country and around the southern end of Lake Michigan into southern Michigan. Already they were occupying lands formerly owned by the Illinois and Miami Indians. They were increasing in numbers and power.

In the French and Indian War the Potawatomi, like most of the tribes of the Northwest, took the side of the French. After the war, when the English had placed garrisons here and there, the Potawatomi joined Pontiac in his conspiracy to drive the English from the Indian lands. They were given the work of capturing Fort St. Joseph near the present Niles, Michigan. They did that with all savage cruelty, massacring eleven of the fifteen soldiers stationed there. They spared the lives of Captain Schlosser and three others whom they took to Detroit and exchanged for Potawatomi prisoners. After the fall of Fort St. Joseph these same Indians then hastened south on the old Indian trail to take part in the capture and massacre at Ft. Miami, now Fort Wayne, May 27, 1763.

*Left* — **Starved Rock as Seen from the River.**
*Right* — **Top of Starved Rock with a fine view of the Ill. River.**

The Potawatomi were much devoted to Chief Pontiac who was from their kindred tribe, the Ottawa. When Pontiac, fleeing from the English, went west he was slain at Kaskaskia, Illinois, by a Kaskaskia Indian. The Kaskaskias were a branch of the Illinois Indians who shielded the one who killed Pontiac. For this reason the Potawatomi, aided by the Miamis and Kickapoo, made war upon the Illinois. It was a war to the death, and the Illinois were almost exterminated in 1765. The last fight was at the rock on the Illinois River, where LaSalle had gathered all these tribes to fight back the Iroquois. In those days the place was known as Fort St. Louis. This large rock rose above the Illinois River more than one hundred feet. The top, which covered almost an acre, could be reached by a difficult path on one side only. Here the last of the Illinois took refuge, but were finally starved into a desperate attempt to escape. Only a few were able to do so. So this picturesque place has been called Starved Rock. Read Osman's most interesting book, "The Last of a Great Indian Tribe."

The Miamis who helped the Potawatomi destroy the Illinois had been for many years the most powerful of the Algonquin tribes in the west. They claimed all of what is now Indiana, the western half of Ohio, the eastern part of Illinois, and the southern part of Michigan. They were a proud race and claimed many rights. After the destruction of the Illinois they quarrelled with their former allies, the Potawatomi and the Kickapoo. In the war that followed, the Miamis were repeatedly defeated and had to retreat to their lands along the Wabash.

After the defeat of the Illinois and the Miamis, the Potawatomi reigned supreme in what is now southern Wisconsin and eastern Illinois, from Milwaukee to the salt licks on the Vermillion River where Danville, Illinois, now stands. On the west they were friendly neighbors to the Kickapoo who had their center on Peoria Lake. Farther north they were in friendly relations with the Sacs and Foxes. On the east they gradually extended their territory into lands once held by the Miamis in northern Indiana and southern Michigan.

Almost from the first the Potawatomi became opponents of the Americans. Although at an earlier period they had assisted Pontiac in his war against the English, they now aided their former enemies in the war with the United States. Because they were farther removed, they did not come into immediate conflict with the Americans as did the Miamis and other tribes. They were ready to fight against the states whenever they could. They had encampments around the Miami village, later Fort Wayne. They joined the Miamis in their raids along the Ohio and in Kentucky. They went hunting in Miami lands south and east of the Wabash. In their first treaty at Fort Harmar, January 9, 1789, they were recognized as having some right to all the lands of the Northwest.

In 'the wars that followed they were active. They took part in the defeat of General Harmar at Kekionga in 1790 and in the massacre of General St. Clair's army at Fort Recovery on November 4, 1791. With other Indian tribes they were defeated at the Battle of Fallen Timbers in August, 1794. They took part in the Treaty of Greenville, August 3, 1795. They were granted one thousand dollars for their claims upon lands ceded to the United States. Among these cessions was one in their territory six miles square at the mouth of the Chicago River. Twenty-four Potawatomi chiefs signed this treaty. Their head chief then was Topenebee whose name was spelled Thu-pen-e-bu.

In the next fifteen years the Potawatomi took part in six different treaties but in none of them were they primarily interested, nor did they lose much land. Most of these treaties had to do with lands lying south and east of the Wabash. But it was quite evident to their chiefs that the time would come when they would have to cede land of their own to the United States. So they came to share in the general dissatisfaction of the tribes in the Northwest Territory.

This dissatisfaction had been growing ever since the wave of immigration westward had begun about the close of the Revolutionary War. While the Indians had welcomed the French traders for a hundred years or more, it was with quite a different feeling that they saw the Americans come pouring into their lands, clearing up the forests and establishing permanent homes. They saw their hunting lands disappearing. They had given expression to this dissatisfaction in the years of attacks upon the settlements along the Ohio and in defeating Harmar and St. Clair. The defeat of the Indians by General Wayne and the Treaty of Greenville somewhat cooled their opposition. Succeeding treaties only showed them that they were destined to lose their homes and hunting grounds to the greedy white men.

The Indian who was to be the leader in opposition to the Americans was the great Shawnee chief, Tecumseh. He and his brother, Tems-kwah-ta-wah, better known as The Prophet, were born in a Shawnee village west of what is now Springfield, Ohio. Later they moved westward and at times were at Greenville, Ohio, and again on White River near Anderson, Indiana. During this time Tecumseh was increasing his opposition to the Indians selling their land to the Americans. To the courageous opposition of Tecumseh, his brother added religious zeal that stirred many Indians into bitter hatred of the Americans. In the spring of 1808 they located on the Wabash River, about two miles below the mouth of the Tippecanoe River. This place had been the site of former Indian villages. It now became a great center for the Indians who were opposed to the Americans. Many Potawatomi were among the prophet's followers.

In 1810 Tecumseh with many followers went to a conference with General William Henry Harrison at Vincennes. Tecumseh was bold and daring. General Harrison was brave and firm. There was almost an open rupture and war at that time. Again in the summer of 1811 Tecumseh approached Vincennes with a large number of Indians. General Harrison, however, was ready to meet him with force. Tecumseh again spoke strongly against the treaties that were being made. Nothing was accomplished. It became more evident that open conflict could not long be avoided.

After this conference Tecumseh went to visit the southern Indians hoping to secure their support. His mother was a Creek and he hoped for help from her tribe. He supposed that there would be no fighting in his absence. But reports of growing hostilities in the north caused General Harrison to march northward with an army of about one thousand men. He came near The Prophet's town on the evening of November 6. The Indians seemed surprised and asked for a conference. Harrison withdrew across the way to higher ground and encamped for the night. Early next morning the Indians attacked with much fury and bravery. The Prophet had promised them a great victory.

On a rock near by he spent his time during the battle in chants and mutterings. Although the Indian force was as large as that of Harrison and had the advantage of making the surprise attack, they were soon driven off. After the battle, General Harrison burned the Indian village and returned with his army to Vincennes.

Several Indian tribes took part in this battle: The Shawnees, Winnebagoes, Kickapoo, and Potawatomi. The Miamis claim they were not in this battle because they were advised by their great chief, Little Turtle, not to join Tecumseh and The Prophet. Just what part the Potawatomi had is difficult to determine. Zachariah Cicott, a half-breed Potawatomi, was one of General Harrison's scouts. On the other hand Abraham Burnett, another half-breed Potawatomi, was one of the leaders in the Indian attack. His name is given to the creek near Harrison's encampment and along which the Indians gathered for the attack. Some claim that the Potawatomi chief, Winamac, led the Indians in the battle. He had, however, been considered the friend of the Americans. There was another Chief Winamac who was a bitter enemy to the whites. It is more likely that he was the Winamac who fought against Harrison. There is no doubt that many Potawatomi were in this battle. Years later, when the first settlers came into Potawatomi lands, they heard many stories from the chiefs and warriors about their part in the battle of Tippecanoe.

# Chapter Two - The Potawatomi at Fort Dearborn

The Battle of Tippecanoe was only an introduction to what is known in history as the War of 1812. As the Potawatomi took an active part at Tippecanoe, so they continued their opposition to the United States in the larger struggle. Within a year they were the leaders in the tragedy known to us as the Massacre of Fort Dearborn.

In 1800 there was no Chicago as we know it today. It is said that during the seventeenth century there had been a strong Miami village there and that powerful chiefs had ruled. But the Potawatomi had driven the Miamis east and south and had occupied the land themselves. Even to them the present site of Chicago was little more than one of the many places where they had camped on their hunting trips. They called it "Checagou," but whether they meant by it a place where skunks live or where wild onions grow has been a question. In either case the name was pronounced as though it had reference to a place that smelled. (Hamilton.) Some, however, declare that the word meant something "big." This, of course, would be in favor with modern Chicagoans.

The first resident of Chicago was a San Dominican Negro who came to this wilderness in 1778 and built a cabin where the Chicago Tribune Tower now stands. His name was Jean Baptiste Pointe de Sable. His name would indicate that he was related to the French. He is said to have been handsome and well educated. For eighteen years this lone Negro lived and traded with the Indians, trading them whisky and other articles for their furs. From 1796 to 1804 the sole resident of Chicago was a Frenchman, Pierre LeMai, and his Indian squaw. In 1804 LeMai sold his establishment to John Kinzie who had been a trader at Detroit and on the St. Joseph River of Lake Michigan. Mr. Kinzie and his family were destined to have a great part in the history of early Chicago.

During the years between the Revolution and the War of 1812, the British never ceased to hope that some day they could win back the Northwest Territory. At Fort Maiden in Canada they maintained a post where many Indians from the Northwest Territory went every year to receive presents and have their hatred of the Americans stirred up. During the early years of the nineteenth century there were many aggravating events that disturbed the Indians. Treaties were being made that were rapidly depriving them of their lands. Tecumseh, the Shawnee orator, statesman, and warrior, was inciting the Indians to rise against the Americans. It was hoped that the Battle of Tippecanoe would show the Indians the hopelessness of their cause, yet in reality it excited them to greater efforts.

President Jefferson, who was much interested in the Northwest Territory, was anxious about its safety. He felt that a military outpost should be established to protect the new frontier. He selected the mouth of the Chicago River as a site for a fort. In the summer of 1803 soldiers arrived to build the fort. At that time there lived at this place Pierre LeMai and his Potawatomi squaw; Mike LePettel, another fur trader; and Antoine Ouilmette and his Indian squaw, Archange. Ouilmette's name is perpetuated in the modern town of Wilmette.

The fort was built on the south side of the Chicago River where Michigan Avenue now crosses. They called it Fort Dearborn, after General Henry Dearborn, secretary of war. The next year John Kinzie came and settled on the north side of the river. His intimate knowledge of and his friendship for the Indians helped the situation very much.

From 1803-1810 Captain John Whistler had command of the fort. Mrs. Whistler and her daughter, Sarah, were the first white women to live in Chicago. Then came Mrs. John Kinzie and her daughter. In 1810 Captain Nathaniel Heald was given command. The next year he went to Kentucky and married Rebekah Wells, daughter of Samuel Wells and a niece of the famous Indian scout, Captain William Wells. Thus there grew up in the future Chicago a small group of women whose opportunities for society were very few and who were constantly surrounded by the perils of the wilderness. The Potawatomi Indians, their neighbors, were curious to see the first white women to come to their country. They continued friendly for several years.

After the Battle of Tippecanoe there was a change in the attitude of the Indians. War with the British seemed certain. Tecumseh was constantly working against the Americans. He and the British had determined that Fort Dearborn was to be one of the first places to be destroyed. The word spread among the Indians, who were ready to receive it. On April 6, 1812, some Winnebago Indians came down the Chicago River and killed two men who, with their families, had settled up the river a few miles. This threw the inhabitants of the frontier post, Fort Dearborn, into excitement and from then on they expected something would happen.

In June, 1812, the United States declared war against Great Britain. But it took weeks for such news to travel from General Hull at Detroit to Fort Dearborn. On August 9, Winamac or Winnemeg, a Potawatomi chief, arrived from Detroit with news from General Hull. The message told Captain Heald of the outbreak of the war, the loss to the Americans of Fort Mackinaw, and gave orders from him to leave Fort Dearborn and attempt to reach Fort Wayne.

Winamac knew what the

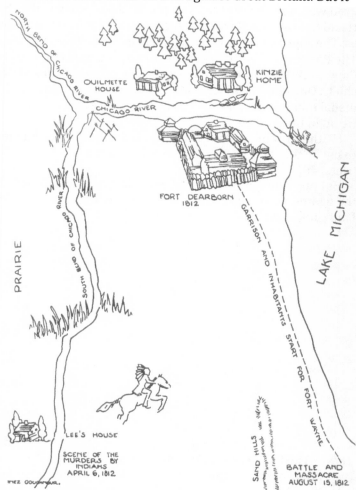

orders were and strongly advised Captain Heald not to comply with them. John Kinzie also advised the captain against leaving the fort and trusting themselves to the wilderness and unfriendly Indians. The Indians seemed to know all about the orders and were soon gathering in large numbers to be on hand when the whites would leave. On August 13 Captain William Wells arrived from Fort Wayne with some friendly Miami Indians. He came because he knew the danger to which the inhabitants of the fort would be exposed,

13

and because Rebekah Wells Heald was his favorite niece. He, too, strongly advised Captain Heald against leaving the fort. But for some reason Captain Heald rejected all advice of those present and determined to carry out the orders of his superior general, William Hull. Arrangements were made to start the perilous journey on the morning of August IS.

The Indians were now in great numbers, estimated as many as five hundred warriors, mostly Potawatomi. On the evening of the thirteenth, Captain Heald held a council with the Indians and made and received certain promises. The captain was to leave the fort and all of its provisions to the Indians. The Potawatomi were to give the Americans safe escort to Fort Wayne. But Captain Wells put no confidence in such promises. Neither did the friendly chiefs. One of them, Black Partridge, came to Captain Heald, bringing to him a medal that had been given him by the Americans. He addressed Captain Heald in these words:

"Father, I come to deliver up to you the medal which I wear. It was given to me by the Americans, and I have long worn it in token of our mutual friendship.

But our young men are resolved to imbrue their hands with the blood of the whites. I can not restrain them, and I will not wear a token of peace while I am compelled to act as an enemy." [1]

*Left* — **The Battle at Fort Dearborn, Aug. 15, 1812. Shown on the southwest pillar of the bridge across the Chicago River on Michigan Avenue.**
*Right* — **Looking North on Michigan Avenue where Fort Dearborn stood and beyond where the Kinzie Home stood on the present site of the Tribune Tower.**

This act of a friendly Potawatomi should have been sufficient to have caused Captain Heald to use the utmost precaution. Then another friendly chief, To-pe-ne-bee, chief of the Potawatomi of St. Joseph River, sent word to his friend, John Kinzie, warning him of the danger and that he should not accompany the garrison from the fort. Mr. Kinzie arranged for his family to go around the lake to St. Joseph with some friendly Indians, but he bravely and generously accompanied the garrison. Captain Wells prepared for the worst. On the morning of the fifteenth he appeared painted in black and in Indian costume, signifying that he was expecting to fight his last.

The morning was beautiful when this train of doomed men, women and children left Fort Dearborn for their march through the wilderness. Least of all did the happy children suspect that their last hour had come. They were happy with the thought of getting out of the closed-in fort and getting an exciting ride through the wilderness. They were on top of one of the wagons filled with goods. Some of the women were in wagons; some were riding beside their husbands on horseback. The company rode down what is now Michigan Avenue, but was then only the lake shore which the waves lapped as if hungry for some prey.

Capt. Wells was constantly on the alert. He rode ahead to see what would happen. Where Monroe Street now goes west from Michigan Avenue, the Indians rode to the west out of sight behind a ridge of sand. Although the company as a whole did not then suspect it, the Indians were preparing an ambush. Captain Wells discovered it and rode back to the company, yelling that they were going to be attacked. At Eighteenth Street, the attack was made.

The battle was soon over. The American militia led by Captain Wells, bravely charged up the sand dunes and did effective work against the redskins. But they were overwhelmed by numbers. Most of the men and some of the women were cut down in the massacre. One young Indian climbed up on a wagon and tomahawked every one of the children except one who was asleep and hidden from view. Captain Wells attempted to save these children in the last fight of his life. Wounded though he was, he rode to their rescue. On his way his horse was shot down and he was pinned under him. He had already killed seven Indians and here he killed another. The Indians surrounded him with mockery, for they had felt his strength in many a fight. He knew they would torture him if he became a prisoner in their hands. The friendly chiefs, Black Partridge and Winamac, attempted to save him, but he preferred death to captivity. To one of the young Indians he yelled: "You are a squaw!" That was too much. Pee-so-tum sank his tomahawk in the captain's brain, tore off his scalp and cut out his heart. The Indians cut it in pieces and ate it, believing that in that way they would acquire some of the characteristics of their brave enemy.

Fifty five of the ninety-six persons who left the fort that morning were slain. Varied and thrilling were the experiences of the few who escaped the massacre. Mrs. Helm was saved by Black Partridge, who prevented an Indian from tomahawking her. Dragging her to the lake, he pretended to be drowning her, whereas he was keeping her away from the Indians until the fury was somewhat over. He then took her to the house of Ouilmette where he hid her till a more opportune time to take her away. Mrs. Heald fought bravely until her body was pierced by several bullets and she fell from her saddle. Even then she used her riding whip on a squaw who attempted to steal her blanket. That night, by the help of some friendly Indians, she and Captain Heald escaped to the Bertrand settlement on the St. Joseph in Michigan. From there the friendly chief, Alexander Robinson, took them to Mackinaw. After being held prisoners for some time at Mackinaw and Detroit, they were released and finally reached their old home in Kentucky. Lieutenant Helm, after being held prisoner at Peoria and Kankakee, was released and finally reached New York where he was joined by his wife. Even the Kinzies, who had many friends among the Indians, came near being massacred. They were rescued by the timely interference of Billy Caldwell and other friendly chiefs. They, too, found safety in flight to the village of Topenebee on the St. Joseph. Many and severe were the hardships endured by those who escaped the massacre.

Within a few days all was quiet where Fort Dearborn once stood. The Indians took whatever they wanted and burned the fort. Most of them took their goods and their prisoners to their villages, but many hastened east to join the forces besieging Fort Wayne, and to follow Tecumseh in the war.

[1] From Waubun, by Mrs. John Kinzie, p. 255.

# Chapter Three - The Potawatomi Cede Their Lands to the United States

The Potawatomi made many treaties with the American government. More than forty such treaties are recorded. Some of them have to do with individuals and small possessions, while others record the cessions of great stretches of territory.

Before the War of 1812 the Potawatomi lost very little land that they could really call their own. They were included in certain treaties which had to do with land they somewhat claimed. After the War of 1812 they hastened to sign a treaty of peace at Greenville, Ohio, July 22, 1814. Sixteen of their leading chiefs signed this treaty. At Spring Wells, near Detroit, September 8, 1815, twenty-four chiefs signed another such treaty. At St. Louis, August 24, 1816, they ceded to the United States a large tract of land in northern Illinois. At the Rapids of the Maumee, near Toledo, September 29, 1817, they ceded most of the land between the Maumee and St. Mary's rivers.

One of the most important of Indian treaties was made at St. Marys, Ohio, in October, 1818. Many Indian tribes took part. The Potawatomi ceded a large tract of land on the west of the Wabash River as far south as the Vermilion River. They were to receive a perpetual annuity of $2,500. At Chicago, August 29, 1821, they ceded a strip of land in northern Indiana. In exchange they were to receive $5,000 annually for twenty years. The Indian families of William Burnett and Joseph Bertrand received many sections. A grant of one section was made on the west side of the St. Joseph River for a school; also a grant of a thousand dollars per year for fifteen years for a teacher. This formed the beginning for the mission school of Isaac McCoy near Niles, Michigan.

At Paradise Springs, Wabash, Indiana, October 16, 1826, the Potawatomi came in large numbers demanding land from the Miamis. They finally agreed to cede all claims south of Eel River to the United States. They also ceded a strip of land north and south through Indiana for the Michigan road. They were to receive an annuity of $2,000 per year for twenty-two years and another $2,000 for education. They also received in goods more than $30,000. The United States agreed to build for them a mill on the Tippecanoe and provide for them a miller. Prominent half-breed families like the Burnetts, Bertrands, Barrons, and Cicotts received many sections of land. Fifty-eight students of the Carey Mission received 160 acres each to assist them in their education.

At the Carey Mission, September 20, 1828, a treaty was made in which the Potawatomi ceded large sections of land in south-western Michigan and north-eastern Indiana. For this they were to receive $2,000 annually. They also received some $25,000 in money from time to time and more than $40,000 in goods. The government was to provide them annually so much for fencing, tobacco, iron, steel, salt, and $1,000 a year for education. At Prairie du Chien, Wisconsin, July 29, 1829, and at Camp Tippecanoe, Indiana, October, 1832, the Potawatomi ceded much land in southern Wisconsin, northern Illinois, and northern Indiana. The Indians were to receive large sums of money annually, some of it promised to them forever. Many reservations were made for prominent chiefs and Indian families.

At Chicago, September 26, 1833, was made the biggest treaty of all between the United States and the Potawatomi. The latter ceded more than 5,000,000 acres in Illinois and Wisconsin and were to receive the same amount of land west of the Mississippi along the Missouri. They were also to receive nearly one million dollars in money and goods. It is interesting to note the large number of Indian families who received special grants in these treaties. These were, for the most part, half-breed families with French or American relatives who helped them secure special favors. Among them are named the families of Billy Caldwell, Alexander Robinson, Joseph Lafrombois. Antoine Ouilmette, William Burnett, Joseph Bertrand, Joseph Bailly, and the Beaubiens, Bourasses, Vieux, Grignons, Chadonis, and others.

This preceding account has been given to show the reader something of the efforts of the United States government to extinguish the Indian title of lands and make it possible for the government to offer it to United States citizens. Many feel that the Indians were dealt with unjustly in being forced to sell their lands and move to the west. Others, even some friends of the Indians, believe that it was the only way to deal with this most serious problem. It would seem as though the government at Washington, for the most part, aimed to deal justly with the Indian, but that often government agents, white settlers and traders did do the Indian great injustice and cheated him out of much he should have had. More and more it became evident that the Indian would lose his ancient domain east of the Mississippi.

The removal of the Indians from the Northwest Territory began early in the nineteenth century. The tribes living in Ohio were the first to be removed. About 1829 the Delawares along White River, Indiana, were taken west. It was not until the thirties that arrangements were made for any large number of Potawatomi to be removed. The Miamis were removed during the forties.

Long before the final removal to the west, the Indian lands were more and more restricted. As white settlers became anxious for more land the Indians were forced to cede large areas, but were given certain reserves. These reserves were often entirely surrounded by the lands taken over by the whites. Most of them were small but some of them quite large, such as the Big Miami Reserve in central Indiana from 1818-1838. The reserves were usually large enough for the family or tribe had they known how to farm, but entirely too small for the Indians' way of making a living by hunting.

From time to time suggestions were made to move the Indians west of the Mississippi. For the most part these suggestions came from those who were greedy for the Indians' land, and were resented by the red men. But in the later twenties, just such a movement was made by one of their trusted friends, the Rev. Isaac McCoy of the Carey Indian Mission near Niles, Michigan. His long experience with the Indians convinced him that there was little hope of doing the Indian much good so long as he was surrounded by white men and exposed to their vices. To interest the government in this movement, McCoy made trips to Washington where he met the leading men of the day. Most of them encouraged him in the project.

In 1828 Rev. McCoy, accompanied by six Indians, three Potawatomi and three Ottawa, made a trip to Kansas and further south to see how the country was suited for the Indian. McCoy was all the more convinced that the Indians should be given homes and lands where they could establish a state with a government suitable to their needs. He soon gave up his work at the Carey Mission and moved to Missouri and later to Kansas. He was engaged as a surveyor and agent by the government. He made a trip almost every year to Washington to interest government officials in his project. He made many trips into the lands south of Kansas and has been called the "Father of Indian Territory."

Two tracts were assigned out west to the Potawatomi. One was in the western Iowa Territory, along the Missouri River just opposite Omaha. Couth cil Bluffs, Iowa, is the county seat of Potawatomi County, Iowa. To this reservation most of the Prairie Potawatomi of Illinois were taken. Arrangements for this move were made at the Treaty of Chicago, September 26, 1833. By 1840 most of the Prairie Potawatomi of Illinois and Wisconsin had gone to their new home.

The other tract of land assigned to the Potawatomi was on the Osage River in eastern Kansas along the Missouri state line. It was near the land assigned to the Miamis. To this place most of the Indiana and Michigan Potawatomi were taken during the late thirties.

This arrangement was not satisfactory to the divided bands of the Potawatomi. Also there was pressure from white settlers for these lands. In June, 1846, there was a treaty made with both bands of the Potawatomi by which they sold their lands in western Iowa and on the Osage River in Kansas for $850,000. The two bands then purchased of the United States a tract of land thirty miles square in north-eastern Kansas. This had been the eastern part of the land that had been reserved for the Kansas Indians. For this land the Potawatomi paid the United States $87,000. The government paid the Indians sufficient to make the move and get settled in their new homes. The balance of the $850,000 was kept by the government as a reserve fund, the interest to be paid to the Indians each year.

In 1861 the Potawatomi were ready for some other arrangement. By a treaty with the United States in 1861, all Indians who so desired and who were deemed competent to handle their own affairs received allotments of their own. Provisions were made for them to become United States citizens. So they are often spoken of as the Citizen Potawatomi. To all the other Potawatomi a reservation was assigned. The size of this reserve would depend upon the number and family position of the Indians. Arrangement was made whereby the Leavenworth and Western Railroad could purchase the lands not assigned to individuals or that were not included in the new reserve. The money paid for this land was held in trust for the Indians by the government.

The last treaty between the Potawatomi and the United States was made at Washington, D. C, February 27, 1867. Provisions were made whereby those who desired could move to Indian Territory, a reservation to be purchased by funds that had accumulated to their credit. This reservation was located on the Canadian River in what is now central Oklahoma, near the Shawnee reservation. Here today is Potawatomi County, Oklahoma, with Shawnee as county seat.

In 1890 the Oklahoma reserve was divided among the members individually. Each Indian was given so much land, which he could dispose of at will. The remainder of the lands were open for white settlers. The result is that the Potawatomi of Oklahoma own very little land today. In trade and dealings with the white men, they were not able to keep their lands. Furthermore, they so intermarried with the white people that there are few full-blooded Potawatomi left. The latest reports indicate more than two thousand Potawatomi in Oklahoma, but most of these have very little Indian blood.

The Potawatomi reservation still continues in Kansas. Those who received individual allotments soon disposed of them and lost most of the money. In more recent years the government is not granting deeds to the Kansas Potawatomi. While each family may live on a farm which they may use as their own, they cannot sell it. The government considers these farms as an Indian reservation with a superintendent to look after their interests. A recent report gives the number of Potawatomi on this reserve to be about one thousand. Mayetta, Kansas, north of Topeka, is the center of their Indian activities.

*Upper* — **Potawatomi Agency Houses, Mayetta, Kansas.**
*Lower* — **Potawatomi Family near Crandon, Wisconsin.**

In Forest County, Wisconsin, there is a Potawatomi reserve, but the Indians have their farms or allotments much the same as those in Kansas. The reserve is near Crandon. Those who reside here are of the branch known as the Forest Potawatomi. In Nebraska, northern Michigan, and in southern Canada are scattered bands of Potawatomi. In southern Michigan, near Hartford, are a few remnants of the Pokagon band. Near Athens, Michigan, is a remnant of the Potawatomi of that section. They have a reserve of 120 acres,, one of the smallest Indian reserves in the country.

# Chapter Four - Menominee and the Trail of Death

Among the Potawatomi who settled in various places in northern Indiana, none has attracted more attention than Menominee and his band who inhabited the country around the lakes a few miles southwest of the present city of Plymouth. The famous Indian missionary, Isaac McCoy, visited Menominee June 11, 1821. At that time his band was small. There were but four small huts where Menominee lived, but not far away were other wigwams and camping places. McCoy's description gives us a good view of the very primitive condition under which these Indians lived — poor huts, cabins and teepees; often poor food, if any at all; and often without any good water to drink. McCoy found Menominee having two wives — sisters — a common practice among the Indians, as Menominee explained.

Menominee had, however, been endeavoring as best he could to lead his people out of savagery and paganism. He had come under the influence of the French Catholic missionaries. He said he had felt a call from the Great Spirit to preach to his people. He had been preaching to his people against the sins of murder, theft, and drunkenness. He showed McCoy a long stick on which he had cut a notch for every sermon he had preached. He was much interested in knowing that McCoy had a little book in which he had recorded the number of sermons he had preached. He had regular hours for worship, and observed Sunday as a time for such worship. These Indians were very devout and attentive at these services. It must have been very interesting to see these two preachers in earnest conversation — the one representing the very best that education and the Christian church could give; the other trying to see the light of truth after having spent so many years in paganism. Menominee very much insisted that McCoy should locate a mission among them, but this missionary had already decided to locate his work among the Potawatomi of southern Michigan.

The Catholic missionaries continued their faithful and effective work among the Indians. As the Indians increased in number, their interest in the Christian religion increased and the result was manifest in their lives. There were fewer instances of murder, theft, and drunkenness than there were elsewhere. After the visit of McCoy, Menominee became very much concerned about the wrongs of polygamy as it existed among them.

About 1827, under the direction of Father Badin, a chapel was built. It was rudely constructed of logs, with a clapboard roof. The timbers were tied together with skins. It was a one-story building but at the west end, over the assembly room, there was a room for the missionary. The room was reached by a ladder only, and had within only the poorest accommodations, but he had books and papers from the best of French libraries. Here was a man educated in the best universities giving his life to help these poor Indians. This chapel was located on one of the many lakes of that region. Though there are a number of lakes in this community, they are referred to as Twin Lakes. The chapel stood on the north bank of one of them about five miles southwest of the present city of Plymouth.

At a treaty made on the Tippecanoe, October 26, 1832 — the United States Commissioners being Governor Jonathan Jennings, John W. Davis, and Mark Crume — twenty-two sections were reserved for the bands of "Men-o-mi-nee, No-taw-kah, Much-kahtah-mo-way, and Pee-pin-oh-waw." At a treaty on Yellow River, August 5, 1836, the last three chiefs named ceded these twenty-two sections to the United States and promised to move to the west within two years. They were to receive for this cession $14,080, but from this amount was to be deducted the amount of debts which certain white men claimed these Indians owed. Menominee did not, and would not, sign this treaty. He would not sell his lands.

In the meantime, the work of the Christian mission at the Menominee chapel continued to grow. In 1837 Benjamin Marie Petit was sent to minister to these Indians. He was only twenty-six years old, but he had already had a brilliant career as a college student, a young lawyer in France, a theological student, and had been ordained to the priesthood. Though a man of much learning and ability, he entered upon his work here with much enthusiasm. His letters were full of praise for his Potawatomi converts and members. He wrote of their religious fervor, their anxiety to know the truth, and of their enthusiasm in getting other Indians to accept Christianity. He called his chapel and mission Chichipe Outipe.

Father Petit reported that there were more than one hundred wigwams and tepees clustered around the chapel, with other villages and encampments not far away. He estimated that there were more than one thousand Indians who had been brought under the influence of the mission. The situation here was quite different from what it was among many other rapidly diminishing Indian settlements where murder, theft, and drunkenness were so common.

But this happy condition was destined not to last very long. Although the treaty reserving this land to the Indians "forever" was less than four years old, there was much pressure from white settlers to drive the Indians westward so they might have the land. Although the treaty which Menominee refused to sign gave the Indians until August, 1838, to move westward, already there were many squatters who had moved in on Indian lands so as to be first when the time expired for the Indians to go. Naturally, this action of the white settlers very much disturbed the Indians, and stirred up much agitation.

When the time arrived, August 5, 1838, for the Indians to move, Menominee refused to do so. Colonel A. C. Pepper, Indian agent, came to Menominee's village and held a council. He tried to induce Menominee and his band to move, in harmony with a treaty which this leader had not signed. In response to Colonel Pepper's demand, Menominee replied in an eloquent address:

"The President does not know the truth. He, like me, has been imposed upon. He does not know that you made my young chiefs drunk and got their consent and pretended to get mine. He does not know that I refused to sell my lands and still refuse. He would not by force drive me from my home, the graves of my tribe, and my children who have gone to the Great Spirit, nor allow you to tell me that your braves will take me tied like a dog, if he knew the truth. My brothers, the President is just, but he listens to the word of young chiefs who have lied. When he knows the truth, he will leave me to my own. I have not sold my lands. I will not sell them. I have not signed any treaty and will not sign any. I am not going to leave my lands and I do not want to hear any more about it."

The final struggle had come, with the outlook very much against the Indians. The white settlers were aggressive and some of them quite unfair to the Indians. One man, who was overanxious to get Indian lands, reported that some Indians had attacked his home and chopped down his door. He and some of his neighbors retaliated by burning down some Indian cabins. Menominee was strong in his resistance and in condemnation of the white men. Colonel Pepper appealed to the government for a force to keep peace. Governor David Wallace appointed General John Tipton to raise the force necessary. It was understood by General Tipton and others that he was to move the Indians to lands west of the Mississippi.

Influenced by exaggerated and one-sided reports of the Indians' conduct, it was easy for Tipton to secure volunteers to remove them. He was soon in their midst with a force of soldiers. Many of the Indians were in the chapel in prayer when the soldiers arrived and gave notice of their presence by a volley of shot. Those who were there were made prisoners and not allowed to return home. How like the famous story of Evangeline! Soldiers were sent out in all directions to bring in others. By September 3, the soldiers had collected 859 Indians, young and old, ready to depart on the morrow.

Father Petit had assembled the Indians in the chapel for their last service. What happened can be gotten from his own words: "I assembled all of my children to speak to them for the last time. I wept and my children sobbed aloud. It was indeed a heart-rending sight, and over our dying mission we prayed for the success of those they would establish in their new hunting grounds. We then with one accord sang 'O Virgin, We Place Our Confidence in Thee.' It was often interrupted with sobs, and few voices were able to finish it." On September 3 they were allowed to visit the little graveyard and hold a final service. The Indians were much attached to the graves of their fathers. It was sad when they gave a last farewell to the resting places of their loved ones.

Of Menominee it was said that his savage nature showed itself in his attempt to defend himself and resist arrest. He stood at bay with a dagger in hand. But the soldiers threw a lasso over his head and bound him hand and foot. He was thrown in a wagon and hauled off from his home and from the work that he had done. He went with his people into captivity. What finally became of him, we do not know.

Sixty wagons had been assembled to transport the women, children, and the aged and infirm. Many of the Indians had ponies, but most of the men had to walk. Before they left on the morning of September 4, the soldiers set fire to all the huts and cabins, so there would be less temptation for the Indians to want to return. But what must have been their feelings to see their homes, which had become so dear to them, go up in smoke? And what must have been their impression of a class of people who claimed to be civilized, many of them professing Christianity?

The experiences of the march may be sensed by the records of General Tipton himself. At the close of the first day he wrote: "September 4, 1838. Left Twin Lakes, Marshall County, Indiana, early this morning. Traveling today was attended with much distress on account of scarcity of water. Provisions and forage were scarce and of poor quality. The distance traveled, twenty-one miles." They spent this first night on the banks of the Tippecanoe, three miles north of Rochester. For September 5, Tipton wrote: "Fifty-one persons were found unable to continue their journey on account of lack of transportation. Most of them were sick, and someone was left to care for them. On account of the difficulties of finding water, a distance of only nine miles was traveled. In the evening a child died and was buried." This evening they encamped at Mud Creek south of Rochester.

The records of the following days were much like this, only worse. At almost every camping place one or more of the Indians were left in nameless graves. Through Logansport and down the Wabash the sad procession continued. Not only was the physical suffering terrible, but the mental anguish was more so. To be driven from the homes of their ancestors and to be on the march hundreds of miles to a land they knew not where nor what were about all human strength could endure. Often these Christian Indians would be seen looking in vain appeal to heaven as if imploring a higher power to help them in their distress.

In fifteen days the march had reached Danville, Illinois. Here General Tipton left them and turned them over to others to continue the journey westward. On across Illinois by way of Springfield and Jacksonville, across the Mississippi at Alton, across the Missouri at Independence, and on to Kansas. They reached the Osage River in eastern Kansas after a march of sixty days. It was now winter time, and without proper shelter or food their terrible sufferings continued.

Mention should be made of the sufferings of Father Petit in behalf of these exiled Indians. Though but a young man yet in his twenties, he had been a sympathetic father to all of his Indian children as they were driven from the homes and graves of their fathers. He was too weak to follow them into exile. But after the march began, so great was the suffering of the Indians that even General Tipton sent back to have Father Petit come and give them comfort. Though unable for the strenuous undertaking, he hastened after them and arrived at their camp Sunday, September 16. He has left us a vivid description of the sufferings of these Indians due to forced marches, dust, lack of water, sickness and mental distress. He continued with them until they reached their new home in Kansas. Here another priest took his place, while he started to return to Indiana. He reached St. Louis, but could go no farther. He was tenderly cared for by his Jesuit brethren. After four weeks of suffering he passed away at the early age of twenty seven, a martyr to the cause of bringing Christianity to the Potawatomi Indians.

In the pioneer efforts to build up an American civilization on lands taken from the Indians, the original owners were all but forgotten. In 1905 Daniel McDonald of Plymouth began a movement to have the state of Indiana do justice to those whom the forefathers had so unjustly treated. By state appropriations and private donations a fine memorial monument was erected in 1909 not far from the original home of Menominee and his band.

*Left* — Monument to Menominee.
*Right* — Marker on the site of Chi-chi-pe Ou-ti-pe.

On the monument is the following inscription: "In memory of Chief Menominee and his band of 859 Potawatomi Indians, removed from the reservation, September 4, 1838, by a company of soldiers under General John Tipton, authorized by Governor David Wallace."

One mile north of this monument and on the site of the Indian Chapel a tablet has been placed on a large boulder near one of the Twin Lakes. The inscription reads: "Menominee Chapel, Chi-Chi-pe Ou-ti-pe, erected by Rev. Theo. Badin, first Catholic priest ordained in the United States, 1793, Succeeded by Rev. Louis De Selle, 1832-1837 and by Rev. Benj. Petit, 1837-1838, when the Indians were removed and the chapel closed."

## Chapter Five - Potawatomi Trails

When the Potawatomi were at the height of their power they had a vast empire in what is now north-eastern Illinois, northern Indiana and southern Michigan. Over this great territory they roamed and hunted. Through this broad land they had some prominent trails and many smaller ones.

The longest of these trails, and perhaps the most important, was known as the Great Sauk Trail. It extended from the mouth of Rock River on the Missis-sippi across Illinois and entered Indiana at about the present city of Dyer on U. S. 30. It passed the present city of Valparaiso and thence northeast near La Porte and entered southern Michigan. It crossed the St. Joseph River at the Pare aux Vaches, or the cow pens as it was called, because in an-cient times there were so many buffalo feeding there. From here the Great

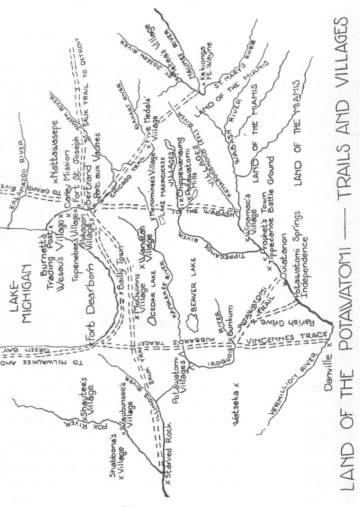

Sauk Trail extended eastward across southern Michigan, passing the sites of the present cities of White Pigeon, Sturgis, Coldwater, Jonesville, Clinton, Ypsilanti, to Detroit. This trail through Michigan later became the route of the Chicago-Detroit road, and is now U. S. 112. Over this route in Indian days, various tribes came and went for the purpose of hunting or war. Over this route Black Hawk often went from his home on the Mississippi to Detroit. Over this route later came thousands of pioneers on their way to western lands. Today thousands of autoists come and go, little thinking of the millions who have gone this way in the past by means of travel from the most primitive to the most modern.

This great route was joined by many others. One of these was from the Green Bay country, Wisconsin, around the southern part of Lake Michigan and on to join the Sauk Trail near Pare aux Vaches. Indian trails led north and south. The most important of these was the one leading southeast to the Miami town of Kekionga, now Fort Wayne. This was the route that led from Kekionga to Chicago. Over this trail William Wells hastened to assist the garrison at Fort Dearborn. The present U. S. 33 approximates it.

From Pare aux Vaches south a trail extended through Indiana. It passed near the Indian settlements on Yellow River and the Tippecanoe. It later became the route of the Michigan road. Along the rivers of northern Indiana and connecting them were many minor trails which were followed by the Potawatomi and other Indians.

The Calumet region of north-western Indiana was a great hunting and camping ground for the Indians. Where now are so many suburban cities of Chicago, the red man once roamed and hunted at will. Important trails passed through this marshy, sandy land just as today railroads go in all directions. There was an important Indian village at what is now Merrillville.

It was first known as Wiggins Point by the white man and later as McGwinn's Village. From this point no less than sixteen trails led off in all directions. One went by the way of present Crown Point, Cedar Lake, and on to Kankakee, Illinois.

The whole of western Indiana and eastern Illinois as far south as the Vermilion River was once a Potawatomi domain with scarcely an intrusion from any other tribe except the friendly Kickapoo. Much of this was then great, grassy prairie. Here the buffalo roamed in countless numbers until 1790. In that year, the Indians say, a very deep snow, some four or five feet deep, covered the whole land. Then rain and a freeze caused the top of the snow to become a glare of ice. During this time the buffalo could find nothing to eat. He could not walk through the ice-covered snow and was too heavy to walk on the top as did many other animals. In this condition the buffalo perished from hunger or were killed by the Indians and predatory animals. Multiplied thousands of them left their bones upon the prairies. The few remaining buffalo seemed to have migrated west of the Mississippi. The land that was once their feeding grounds became the hunting grounds of the Indians and later the homes of prosperous farmers.

Through this great prairie ran one of the most important trails in the Northwest. It was at first known as the Vincennes Trace, for it extended north from Vincennes to Chicago through the heart of the Indian country. Vincennes was the most important city in the Northwest for many years. From it many trails led southward to various points on the Ohio River. One of these was the Buffalo Trace over which countless buffalo made their way from the feeding grounds of the prairies to the salt licks and grassy pastures of Kentucky.

**Big Potawatomi Springs, Independence, Indiana, on the Wabash River.**

The trace northward was mostly in what is now Illinois, but near the state line. It passed through the present city of Danville on the Vermilion River of the Wabash. It led northward through the present city of Sheldon. Here it was joined by an important Potawatomi trail from the southeast. This trail started at the Potawatomi Springs near the present city of Attica. It ran north through Warren and Benton counties, Indiana. At Parish Grove it was joined by another trail which led to the Wea Towns and to The Prophet's Town on the Wabash. The combined trails led northwest to join the Vincennes Trace at Sheldon. From here the Vincennes Trace led northward through Iroquois, Donovan and on to Chicago.

Over this trail the Potawatomi and Winnebago warriors went south to confer with Tecumseh and to take an important part in the Battle of Tippecanoe. Northward over the same route the Wabash Potawatomi hastened to take part in the massacre of Fort Dearborn. Along this route, from Danville to Chicago, Gurdon Hubbard later established trading posts so that the Vincennes Trace became known as Hubbard's Trace. It became a great pioneer road for emigrants to the west. Thousands of moving vans and caravans went to their homes in the northwest by this route from the Ohio River. It was one of the first routes to be improved by the state of Illinois.

In its early pioneer days this route was dangerous to travel. Here and there in this great prairie were low hills or groves which afforded good places for camping. But some of these pleasant looking places became the rendezvous for robbers who went forth to rob and kill the travelers. From this trace other trails led off to hunting grounds and to places where banditti had their centers.

The Kankakee River was a great highway for the Potawatomi. Only a few miles of portage near present South Bend connected the Kankakee and its outlet to the Mississippi with the St. Joseph and its outlet to the great lakes and the St. Lawrence. Along this water route LaSalle and many other explorers and traders made their way to the Illinois and Mississippi. The Illinois River and its important tributaries, the Fox, the Des Plaines, and the Kankakee, were highways of travel for the Potawatomi. Every river and creek was a route for their canoes or dugouts. Almost every community once had traditions of some Indian trail along a creek, river, or across country to some other land trail or water route.

These trails were valuable not only to the Indians in their day but to the pioneers who came by wagon or horseback to their new homes in the wilderness. The early county and state routes often followed these trails. Even today many of our prominent paved highways follow these trails. We follow the pathway not only of our pioneers but of the red men who preceded them.

# Chapter Six - The Potawatomi of the Wabash Along the Ke-na-po-co-mo-co and the Tip-pe-ca-noe

The Potawatomi were often spoken of as having three territorial divisions: The Potawatomi of the Wabash, The Potawatomi of the St. Joseph, and The Prairie Potawatomi.

The Potawatomi coming south from the Wisconsin territory around Lake Michigan and also from northern Michigan entered what is now Indiana. A large increase in their numbers, pressure from other tribes, and perhaps an invitation from the Miamis explain this movement. Or it may be that the Potawatomi just moved into Miami territory and crowded them southward. The Miamis moved the center of their activities to the important village called Ke-kion-ga, where the city of Fort Wayne now stands. The Potawatomi followed closely. Along the Tippecanoe they had many villages and later many reserves. They continued southward until they reached that important tributary of the Wabash known to the Miamis as the Ke-na-po-co-mo-co, but in present day geography as Eel River. Ke-na-po-co-mo-co is a Miami word meaning snake fish. Along the northern bank of this river the Potawatomi built their villages. They did not cross, in any large numbers at least, for on the south side of this river the Miamis had their villages and were ready to repel the invaders.

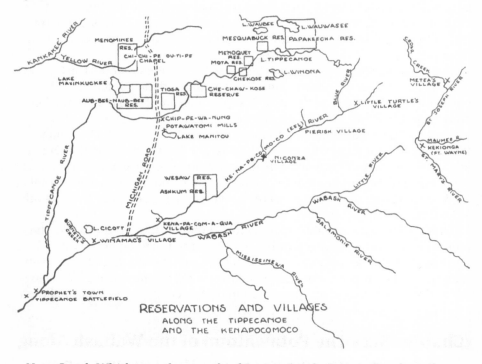

RESERVATIONS AND VILLAGES
ALONG THE TIPPECANOE
AND THE KENAPOCOMOCO

Near South Whitley, at the mouth of Spring Creek, George Croghan, the English traveler, witnessed a great gathering of Potawatomi Indians for their green corn dance in 1765. On what is now the campus ground of Manchester College there was a large village. The last chief was Pierish. Early settlers would point out his grave, and many relics give evidence of this Indian village. Close to Stockdale on the boundary line between Wabash and Miami counties, a Potawatomi chief, Niconza, had a village. The English translation of his name was Squirrel. So he was known to the early settlers as Captain Squirrel. Both of his names were perpetuated by the names of Niconza post office and Squirrel Creek. Captain Squirrel had married a Miami woman. So after the Potawatomi had ceded their land along the Kenapocomoco to the United States, Captain Squirrel moved to a reserve in Miami territory near what is now Bunker Hill.

Near Denver, Indiana, were two Potawatomi reservations. Here as late as 1836 Chief Ashkum received as a reserve sixteen sections and Chief Wesaw four sections. These lasted but a short time, when they were receded to the United States and the Potawatomi moved to the west.

Farther down the river, however, the Miamis still held ground on the north side of the Kenapocomoco. Near later Adamsboro was the important Miami village of Ke-na-paw-com-a-qua. Captain Wilkinson was sent from

30

Cincinnati with an array of cavalry to destroy it in September, 1791. Later it was rebuilt and for years was an important center of Indian life and gatherings. It was known to early settlers as Old Towne. The site of the village and battlefield may still be pointed out six miles up Eel River from Logansport.

On the upper course of the Kenapocomoco the Miamis held full sway. It would seem that the Potawatomi never got farther southeast than the Blue River branch of Eel River. Five miles east of the present Columbia City, was the village and ancestral home of the great chief, Little Turtle. He held full sway in the triangle north of Eel River and east of Blue River. In the territory on Eel River south of Columbia City on what was known as the Island, Little Turtle kept a garrison of warriors to be ready to repel any surprise attacks of the Potawatomi. In the western part of Whitley County, conflicts between these two tribes of Indians were common. Between the Little Turtle village on the upper course of Eel River and the historic village, Ke-na-paw-com-a-qua, on the lower course of the river, was a great hunting country. All accounts indicate that the Eel River country was one of the best hunting grounds in Indiana. The Miamis dealt much in furs which they collected at their trading post near the Turtle village, ready to portage them across to Kekionga. Eel River was a highway of trade and travel. Along its course Little Turtle often made trips between the two important Miami villages still remaining on the north side of the Kenapocomoco. But along the remaining north side of the river the Potawatomi held sway.

The Tippecanoe was a Potawatomi river. Along its banks were located a number of Potawatomi reservations and villages. The name of the river is derived from the Potawatomi word, Ke-tap-i-kon, or Ke-tape-kon-nong, meaning the place of buffalo fish. The water of this beautiful river is the clearest of any river in the state. It flows out from a beautiful lake and by many lakes, yet the Indians preferred to build their villages along its banks rather than by the side of a lake. Beginning on its upper course where it flows out of Lake Tippecanoe, we will notice the various villages with their chiefs.

West of Lake Tippecanoe, four sections of land were reserved for Chief Mes-qua-buck and his band, October 27, 1832, at a treaty made on the Tippecanoe River. The village of this chief was near the site, of the present village of Oswego. When the white settlers first came there were about 125 Indians here. The old chief was a mild-mannered Indian, and was generally known as a friend of white men. One old settler said he was the best friend that he ever had. Mesquabuck had four sons. Two of them were twins, with the names Macose and Mazette. Another son, John, was quarrelsome and was killed in a fight near Leesburg. The youngest son, Bill, was a favorite with the whites. The Indians were left on their reservation but a short time. In March, 1836, they were forced to give up the reserve and move to the west. The chief and his people were given one dollar per acre, or $2,560. They were to move within two years. The old chief, already heartbroken because of the prospective move, was killed by a fall from a horse.

Three miles north of Warsaw, where the present state route IS crosses the Tippecanoe, there was the largest of these Tippecanoe villages. Here Men-oquet was chief. The early whites estimated the number of Indians in this village to be 150. Menoquet, like many of these Potawatomi chiefs, fought against the Americans in the Battle of Tippecanoe. But whereas Mesquabuck and others became reconciled and friendly, Menoquet never did. He was morose and sullen and much given to drink and quarrels. His death took place a few days after a night of carousal in which a young Indian squaw from a northern tribe took part. His people began to suspect that she had be-

**Chief Menoquet - *Courtesy Eli Lilly***

witched him. When she heard of their suspicions she attempted flight. Two young braves pursued her and tomahawked her at the edge of a swamp one mile south of the present Leesburg. Early settlers know the place as the spot where the Indian princess met her death.

Menoquet was buried with pomp and ceremony. He was set upright against a tree in the small field just south of the present Menoquet bridge. His horse and dog were killed and placed beside him. Hunting arms and food were placed by his side and a fence of branches was built about to keep it from being disturbed. But the few white men in the country would not permit such a condition to remain, and set fire to the whole. Here on the site of the old Indian village, the pioneers built the village which they named Menoquet after the old chief.

Menoquet had received his four sections at a treaty made on the Tippecanoe River, October 27, 1832. It was ceded to the United States at a treaty made at the Tippecanoe village, Chip-pe-wa-nung, September 23, 1836. The price paid to the Indians was $1.25 per acre, and they were to remove west of the Mississippi within two years. Menoquet did not sign this treaty, and it is altogether likely he had gone to the happy hunting grounds in the manner already described.

West of the present city of Warsaw, along U. S. 30, on either side of the Tippecanoe River were the reservations of Chekose and Mota. Each consisted of four sections granted to these chiefs at the treaty of October 27, 1832.

Chekose was a keen trader with the whites, and a match for them at times. Mota was known to early settlers for being disfigured by the loss of a part of his nose. These villages were quite small. Mota and his band ceded this reserve back to the United States in December, 1834, and agreed to move soon to their home west of the Mississippi. The government paid the old chief and his tribe $600.

North of Atwood, near Clunette, was the home of Chief Benack. He was a bitter enemy of the white man. He boasted that he had ninety-nine tongues that he had cut from the mouths of white men and he wanted one more. When told by some of the old pioneers that if he did not shut up, his own tongue would make the one hundredth he ceased to boast. But he must have had much influence with the white men, for he received a number of land cessions. In one treaty he received eight sections and his daughter received three. This daughter, Mary Ann, had married an Irishman, Edward McCarty. Benack did not like his son-in-law. So he had his daughter give her husband a section of land to leave her.

**Site of Potawatomi Mills, Lake Manitou.**

On the Tippecanoe near the present town of Tippecanoe, Chief Che-chaw-kose received ten sections for himself and his band in 1832. Here the Catholics had a mission for a time. But like most of these Tippecanoe reserves, this one lasted but a few years. In 1836 the land was ceded to the United States and the Indians agreed to move west within two years. They received $8,000 for their land, but agreed to pay all debts to the white traders. These debts were always large, and there is "just suspicion that they had been padded, for the Indian never kept any account for himself."

At the treaty made at Paradise Springs on the Wabash, 1826, the United States agreed to build a mill on the Tippecanoe River and support a miller for the benefit of the Potawatomi. This mill, however, was not built on the river, but at the outlet of Lake Manitou in the eastern part of the present city of Rochester. John Lindsey moved here with his family to build and care for the mill. Mrs. Lindsey was afraid to come because of the Indians. She found disease a worse enemy, for she soon died of a fever. She was the first white person to be buried within the present limits of Rochester. Near the mill was a blacksmith shop conducted by Nathan Rose. This mill must not have been used very much, for in 1834 the Potawatomi ceded the two sections of land at the mill and released the government from further responsibility.

*Upper* — **Tippecanoe River at Chippewanung.**
*Lower* — **Where the Michigan Road crosses the Tippecanoe and the site of Chippewanung.**

Chippewanung was the site of a village on the Tippecanoe where the old Michigan road, now U. S. 31, crosses the river three miles north of Rochester. This was also known as Camp Tippecanoe. Here nine different treaties were made between the Potawatomi and the United States. More land changed hands here than at some better known treaty places.

Here today is a large boulder on which is this inscription:

Site of Indian Village
Chip-pe-wa-nung
1836
Where treaties were signed which transferred
The Potawatomies
From this territory to land in the west.
Here soldiers camped with one thousand Indians
On removal of the last Potawatomies
In 1838.

North of this place, along U. S. 31, there were a number of reserves with much the same history as those along the river. The Indians were given assurance of having these lands as theirs forever, but from four to six years was as long as they were left undisturbed. Toiso, Memotway, and Mesack were the minor chiefs in this region.

34

The most prominent chief of this section was Aubbee-naub-bee. For twenty years or more he was active in Indian affairs and signed some of the most important treaties. In 1832 he received a reserve of thirty-six sections for himself and his band. It lay in the northern part of the present Fulton County, and near the Marshall County line.

This old chief was brave, but very gruff and disagreeable. At one treaty he would speak and dared any other chief to contradict him. Even the brave old chief, Waubunsee, respected his daring words. He was mean to his family, and on one occasion killed one of his squaws. His tribe met and condemned him to death. They appointed his son, also the son of the murdered woman, to kill his father. The son seemed to be willing, for then he would become chief. He soon found his father intoxicated and killed him. Aubbeenaubbee is said to have been buried a little northwest of the Richland Center public school. Soon after the United States agents made a treaty with this son, Pau-koo-shuck. The tribe was paid $23,040 for their lands, and agreed to move west within two years. One unique thing about this treaty is that it was signed by six men and six women. Indian women did not usually sign treaties.

One other chief deserved attention. On the east side of Lake Maxinkuckee a chief by the name of Nauswaugee had three sections of land. He ceded his land to the United States on April 22, 1836, and agreed to move west within two years. Although the whites had no right to be in this territory before the expiration of the two years, many of them did come in as "squatters," ready to get land at the first legal chance. They found this old Indian very agreeable and learned to like him. When the time came for him to leave, he took one more walk along his beloved lake and took one more look at his home and his lands. Then he called his white neighbors in and gave them this touching address:

"My white brethren, I have called you here to bid you farewell. Myself and my band at sunrise tomorrow move on to an unknown country that the government of the United States has provided for us west of the Missouri. I have sold my lands and agreed to move within two years. The time is about to expire, so we leave you and the scenes so dear to us all. The white settlers have been good to us and it seems like severing the ties of friendship. We go away never to return. We go away remembering you with kindness." — Quoted from a paper by Mrs. Frank Sterner.

This address is said to have brought tears to many of the pioneer settlers who heard him. Each one must have felt some sting of conscience, for it was the pressure of the white men for Indian lands that had caused just such scenes as this. The next morning the chief with the members of his band mounted their ponies with their belongings and moved off towards the setting sun.

Along the lower course of the Tippecanoe were villages and encampments here and there at what is now Buffalo, Monticello, and other places. Almost every community has some record of such village sites. The old pioneers found much evidences of these by the Indian relics, mostly the arrow and spearheads which they called flints. George Cicott had a reserve near the lake that bears his name. Chief Winamac had his village eleven miles southwest of Logansport on the Wabash. The land he claimed became the reserve of Abraham Burnett. More will be said of these reserves in a later chapter.

## Chapter Seven - The Potawatomi of the St. Joseph In Northern Indiana and Southern Michigan

So far as our American history goes, Northern Indiana and Southern Michigan have been Potawatomi lands. However, when LaSalle and his companions, the first white men to enter the state, came by canoe up the St. Joseph River from Lake Michigan to the present site of South Bend, the Miami Indians lived there. LaSalle named the river the Miami and the first fort at the mouth of the river was called Fort Miamis. The conflict that came between the Miamis and the Potawatomi in eastern and northern Illinois about 1765 soon spread eastward and the Potawatomi entered this Miami country. In the course of time the Potawatomi drove the Miamis southward to the Eel River tributary of the Wabash. So when the Americans first arrived the Potawatomi were in possession of this country and their names had already been given to many places.

The St. Joseph River is largely a Michigan river and will be noted later. The Kankakee was connected with the St. Joseph by a portage of only a few miles. Both the Miamis and the French had used this connection between Lake Michigan and the Illinois River. Then came the Potawatomi who used the Kankakee not only for hunting but for trade and travel as well. The name probably comes from the Potawatomi word Ki-a-ki-ki, which means swampy country. While too swampy for villages on its banks, yet near by were villages, so that the Indians would not be far away from good fishing and hunting. Wanatah's village was in the southern part of the present Starke County. Tassinong's village was in the southern part of the present Porter County. Mes-kwah-ock-bi's village was in the southern part of the present Lake County on Cedar Lake, which was a favorite camping place for the Potawatomi. In the Calumet region and farther east were Indian camping places and early white trading posts.

South of the Kankakee River in Newton County there was once a lake, some seven miles long and five miles wide. It was not very deep and here and there were islands which afforded homes for wild animals. The place was known as Beaver Lake, for it seemed to have countless numbers of this famous fur-bearing animal. There were many other game and fur-bearing animals. Its waters abounded in fish, while wild fowls were there by the million.

It was a real paradise and a happy hunting ground for the Indian.

The great prairie stretching for a hundred miles south from the Kankakee in western Indiana really belonged to the land of the Prairie Potawatomi of Illinois, but is mentioned here with the Indiana lands. Here and there throughout this large territory were camping places for the Indians, not only the Potawatomi but also their friendly neighbors, the Kickapoo.

One of the most noted of their villages was near the present city of Morroco, Newton County, Indiana. Here a minor Potawatomi chief, Turkey Foot, had his den and went forth to plunder and murder. Many a theft and murder was later traced to him. He even went across the Mississippi to secure plunder. His end came in a very fitting way. Another Potawatomi chief, Bull Foot, came to visit him. Both became drunk and in their spree Bull Foot was killed by Turkey Foot, who, in turn, was killed by the son of Bull Foot. They disposed of the two chiefs by placing their bodies in sitting position against near-by trees. About them they placed their war trinkets and many other things which the Indian thought necessary for them in the happy hunting grounds. Around it all they built a pen of brush and logs to keep out the wolves and dogs. Years later the white settlers found the bones of these old Indians.

The Elkhart River is the chief tributary to the St. Joseph. Near the mouth of this river, at the present city of Goshen, was the village Elk Heart, or Me-shehwah-ou-deh-ik in the Potawatomi language. This is not the name of a chief, but was suggested by the shape of an island near the mouth of the river.

On the upper course of the river was the village of the famous Potawatomi chief, Onaxa, or Five Medals. There has been some question as to whether his village was in Elkhart or in Noble County. The best evidence suggests that it was in the present Elkhart County, west of the town of Benton. Five Medals was a powerful chief and a friend to the great Miami chief, Little Turtle. He joined with Little Turtle in writing the following letter to the Quakers of Baltimore:

Little Turtle's Town, Sept. 18, 1803.

Brothers and friends of our heart, we received your speech from the hand of our friend, William Wells, with the implements of husbandry you were so kind to send in his care, all in good shape.

Brothers, it is our wish that the Great Spirit will enable you to render to your red brethren that service which you appear to be so desirous of doing them and which their women and children are so much in need of.

Brothers, we will try and use these articles you have sent us and if we should want more we will let you know.

Brothers, we are sorry to say that the minds of our people are not so much inclined towards the cultivation of the earth as we could wish them.

Brothers, our Father, the President of the United States, has prevented traders from selling liquors to our people, which was the best thing he could do for his Red Children.

Brothers, our people appear dissatisfied because the traders do not as usual bring them liquor, and we believe will request our Father to let the traders bring them liquor, and if he does your Red Brethren are lost forever.

Brothers, you will see from what we have said that our prospects are bad at present, though we hope the Great Spirit will change the minds of our people and tell them that it is better for them to cultivate the soil than to drink whisky.

Brothers, we hope the Great Spirit will permit some of you to come and see us, when you know better whether you can do anything for us.

Brothers, we delivered to you the sentiments of our hearts when we spoke to you at Baltimore and shall say nothing more at present. We now take you by the hand and thank you for the articles you were so kind to send us.

Little Turtle, Miami Chief.<br>
Five Metals, Potawatomi Chief.

The Friends Meeting received this letter and sent a young man, Philip Dennis, to teach the Indians agriculture. His work, begun on the Wabash River in the spring of 1804, was the first effort to teach agriculture in the state of Indiana.

Chief Shipshewana had a village near the village that now bears his name. Near Howe, Indiana, was a village of importance for trade and Indian gatherings. It was called Mon-go-quin-ong. Farther east there were Indian camping places and some small villages, but none of great importance. In the northeast part of Indiana, where now is the Pokagon State Park and the famous Potawatomi Inn, the Potawatomi Indians seldom went except for hunting. Around Hamilton, Steuben County, there are evidences of either early Indians or mound builders.

The only Potawatomi village in eastern Indiana of importance was that of Metea at the mouth of Cedar Creek on the St. Joseph River. We will have more to say about him later.

While the Potawatomi occupied practically all of northern Indiana south as far as Eel River, there were two Miami chiefs who did not give up their land to the invaders. They were Papakeecha and Wauwasee. They seem to have been brothers, and worked together to hold their land. Papakeecha signed the treaty of St. Marys in 1818. He often signed his name as Flat Belly. Both of them signed the treaty made at Paradise Springs on the Wabash at what is now the city of Wabash, October 23, 1826. At that treaty Papakeecha was granted thirty-six sections of land in what is now the northeast part of Kosciusko County and the northwest part of Noble County. The government also agreed to build each of them a house not to exceed six hundred dollars each.

Wauwasee had his village near the southeast corner of what is now Lake Waubee, southeast of Milford, Indiana. The early maps call this Lake Wauwasee. When the larger lake to the east, formerly called Turkey Creek Lake, was given the name Wauwasee, the smaller lake to the west was given the name Waubee. Waubee is but a contraction of Wauwasee, and it is quite certain that this was the home of the old chief. The course of the race track, the council grounds and other evidences of Indian life are pointed out today.

Papakeecha had his village some ten miles east of his brother. About one-mile northwest of Indian Village, Noble County, may be seen some remains of the old brick house which the government built for Papakeecha. But where was the house the government promised to build for Wauwasee? And why did the treaty give so much land to Papakeecha and none to his brother? Is it likely that the government gave the two brothers this large section of land in common, but mentioned only the name of the older, who might have been considered chief? Tradition says that the brick house on the Papakeecha reserve was a double brick house. Is it likely that Wauwasee living so far west from his brother and so near the Potawatomi chiefs on the Tippecanoe preferred to move closer to his brother? There they were closer to the Miami villages on Blue River and Eel River. There are well known trails leading from the Papakeecha reservation to the Miami villages to the south. At a treaty made at the Forks of the Wabash, near Huntington, in 1834, these two Miami chiefs ceded their land to the United States.

There is no record of what became of Wauwasee. It is not likely that either of the chiefs lived very long after being deprived of their land. One story is that Papakeecha took to drinking heavily. One day after he had drunk too much of the white man's firewater he started across the lake that bears his name, in a canoe. He there undertook to do one of his Indian dances in the canoe, and went to the happy hunting grounds by the water route.

The southern part of Michigan was Potawatomi land. One of the most thickly settled portions of their domain was in the triangle included within the St. Joseph River and Lake Michigan. Near the mouth of the St. Joseph was the Burnett trading post where once stood Fort Miamis of LaSalle. Near the Indiana line, at Pare aux Vaches, was the trading post of Joseph Bertrand and not far to the north was the village of the great chief, To-pe-ne-bee, father-in-law of Bertrand and brother-in-law of Burnett. Southwest of Bertrand two miles was the Pokagon village. Farther down the river on the east side was the site of Fort St. Joseph. Opposite the present city of Niles was the Carey Mission where Isaac McCoy tried to help these people. North of him were the villages of Weasau and Macousin. Through this triangle ran the Great Sauk Trail from Chicago to Detroit. With the advantages of trail, river and lake, this section was of great value to both Indians and early white men. Much could be written about the history of this land. Much is given in other chapters of this volume.

There was a close relationship between the Potawatomi and the Ottawa. The dividing line between them, both as to blood and territory, was not clearly defined. The Ottawa claimed most of the southern peninsula of Michigan south to the Kalamazoo. In the territory south of this river, the Potawatomi lived and hunted. Near the present city of Kalamazoo once stood the village of Match-e-be-nash-she-wish. This and another small reserve not far away, called Prairie Ronde, were ceded to the United States in 1827.

North of the present city of Sturgis, Michigan, was the reservation known as the Nottawa Sepa. Some say that the two words mean "a prairie along the river." J. B. Dalby, a Delaware Indian who speaks the Potawatomi language, says it means "the river of the Ottawa." It was definitely set apart in 1821 and reaffirmed in 1832. But on September 27, 1833, this tract was demanded and receded to the United States. It is said that a French trader, Moreau, came into this section in an early day, married a Potawatomi squaw and by her had seven children. The oldest was Sauaquet, who succeeded his father about 1830. He was chief of the tribe when the final transfer was made. These Indians were very angry about the loss of their lands and Sauaquet was murdered by one of his own tribe. The towns of Nottawa and Waseppi, and Nottawa Road through Sturgis, Michigan, remind us of these Indians. At the site of Coldwater was the Mickesawbe reserve which was ceded to the United States in 1827. Along the old Sauk Trail were smaller settlements of Potawatomi, but none of importance in eastern Michigan. There was at one time a Potawatomi village near Detroit, but it was of little importance and did not last long.

*Left* — Site of Fort St. Joseph near Niles, Michigan.
*Right* — Monument of Chief White Pigeon.

One of the stories that has come down to us from pioneer days is that of Wabememe, or White Pigeon. He was friendly to the whites. He attended an Indian council near Detroit where the Indians planned to massacre the early white settlers along the old Sauk Trail. He started out to warn his friends who had begun the settlement at White Pigeon, Michigan, one of the oldest towns in the state. He ran most of the way, fording streams and swamps. He warned his white friends of their danger, but the strain was too great even for his strong heart. He fell dead and is buried west of White Pigeon. Today there is a large stone marker at the junction of U. S. 112 and U. S. 131. On this marker is this inscription: "In memory of Wabememe, Chief White Pigeon, who about 1830, gave his life to save the settlement at this place." The town of White Pigeon and the Pigeon River are also memorials to this Potawatomi Indian.

Two small groups of Potawatomi Indians remain in southern Michigan. One is the remnant of the Pokagon band. They do not have a reservation of their own, but live in scattered groups near the present cities of Dowagiac, Hartford, and Cassapolis.

Near Athens, Michigan, is a small reservation of 120 acres. Here a remnant of the Potawatomi live in comparative peace and comfort. They raise much of what they need for food. They supplement their small farm income by work where they can secure it. They have a church of their own and seem to take much interest in religious work. Their children attend the public schools of Athens where they are making good records. While this reservation is generally known as the Athens Indian Reserve, Albert Mackety. one of the leaders, says the official name is "Nottawa Seppe Pottawattomie Indian Reserve."

*Upper* — **Potawatomi girls in the Athens High School.**
*Lower* — **The Potawatomi Church on the main road through the Athens Indian Reserve.**

# Chapter Eight - The Prairie Potawatomi In Northern Illinois and Southern Wisconsin

There has been considerable discussion about the relationship of the names "Potawatomi" and "Mascoutens." There is no intention here to discuss the matter more than to give some well-known explanations. The usual explanation of the term "Potawatomi" is "People of the Place of Fire." The most common explanation of the term "Mascoutens" is "People of the Little Prairie." With due regard to other explanations this one seems best: That the name "Mascoutens" was first applied to a small group of the Potawatomi who

41

left the main tribe of the Potawatomi in Wisconsin and moved south to the prairie country of southern Wisconsin and northern Illinois. As others moved southward this term became applied to them also. In time the larger group of the Potawatomi were those in the prairie country and were also called "Mascoutens." So the name is often applied to the whole tribe of the Potawatomi. But since the Potawatomi of the prairie are so different from the Potawatomi of the northern forests, they came to distinguish them as the Prairie Potawatomi and the Forest Potawatomi. It is with the former that our history mainly deals. The Forest Potawatomi did not come in touch with the Americans as much as the Prairie band.

Just when the Mascoutens came into the prairies is not certain. No doubt their coming was gradual, but they grew rapidly. By 1765 they had become so powerful that by the aid of the Kickapoo and the Miami they were able to challenge the powerful Illinois and practically destroy them. Then in turn they drove the Miamis to the east out of the prairie country. They were more closely related to the Kickapoo and were on friendly terms with them. They lived in great numbers along the north side of the Illinois opposite Starved Rock, between the present cities of LaSalle and Morris. The present village of Utica was the center of their camps and villages.

The upper Illinois and its tributaries, the Fox, the Des Plaines and the Kankakee, were Potawatomi streams. On the prairies north of Morris was the village of Chief Shabbona. He was one of the most admirable of all Potawatomi chiefs. His own village at Shabbona Grove and the near-by village of Assiminekon at Paw Paw Grove were on the western fringe of the Potawatomi settlements. Along the Fox River were a number of small villages, chief of which were the village of Shaytee near the present city of Geneva and that of Waubunsee at Aurora.

There has been some question as to where Waubunsee lived, but the Aurora historians claim that it was where their city now stands. This chief was a combination of some admirable traits with some of the most savage. He was daring and knew no fear. He avenged himself for the death of a friend at the hand of the Osages by boldly entering a village at night and securing a scalp. He was a willing and active supporter of Tecumseh. When General Harrison was going up the Wabash, Waubunsee boldly climbed into one of the boats and killed a soldier. He was on hand for the massacre of Fort Dearborn, but used his influence against the slaughter of the white people. He was war chief of the Potawatomi and took an active part in the War of 1812. He signed the treaty of peace at Greenville, Ohio, in 1814, and always kept the peace. To show his loyalty to the United States he joined the American army against Black Hawk in 1832. He signed the treaty made at Wabash in 1826 and another at the Carey Mission in 1828. He signed away his lands at the Treaty of Chicago in 1833. He made a trip to Washington in 1835 to see the Great White Father, the President of the United States. While here he had his picture painted by King. It shows him to be a vigorous character. He moved with his people to Council Bluffs, where he died.

Another chief of this section was Black Partridge. We know him best for having saved the life of Mrs. Helm in the massacre of Fort Dearborn. His village was on the Illinois River. He went west and some of his descendants are living in the Kansas Potawatomi reserve today.

The Kankakee River was a great Potawatomi highway of trade and travel. While the Kankakee lands of Indiana were low and swampy, the Kankakee of Illinois had higher banks more suited for villages. The Potawatomi called it the wonderful river and had many more or less permanent villages along its course. Rock Village and Little Rock were best known. Other villages located near the present city of Kankakee and named in U. S. treaties were Meshketeno, Muskwawasepeton, Waisuscuck, and Soldiers.

The Vincennes Trace passed through the entire length of the Potawatomi lands from Chicago southward. That and the Iroquois River, tributary to the Kankakee, were courses for trade and travel. Along this route Gurdon Hubbard established trading posts, so that the northern part of the route became known as Hubbard's Trace. Watseka perpetuates the name of Hubbard's Potawatomi wife. The western part of Indiana belonged to the Mascoutens or Prairie Potawatomi, but has already been described with the lands of the Potawatomi living in the present state of Indiana.

Milwaukee, one hundred miles north of Chicago, was on the border between the Forest Potawatomi to the north and the Mascoutens, or Prairie Potawatomi, to the south. Early travelers and missionaries noted its favorable position for trade. The name is of Potawatomi origin meaning "rich and beautiful land." Both English and French traders bartered with the Indians at an early age. Alexander La Framboise came here about 1784. Jacques Vieau settled here in 1789. Most of these early traders married Indian women and raised Indian families. In 1818 Solomon Juneau came as an employee of Jacques Vieau. He married Vieau's daughter, Josette. Juneau and his wife had great influence over the Potawatomi Indians. He was the leading citizen in the early days of Milwaukee and in course of time became very rich.

Milwaukee was on the Indian trail that led from Green Bay to Chicago. Between Milwaukee and Chicago there was scarcely an Indian village of any importance. But the country was a great hunting region controlled by the Potawatomi. As in modern times so in the early days there was much trade and travel between these important places.

Chicago was first known to early travelers, traders and missionaries as a Miami village. After the Miamis were driven to the east, the Potawatomi were all powerful in that neighborhood. It was with them that the early traders of Chicago such as the French Negro, Baptiste Point Sable, Jean B. La Lime, Pierre LeMai, and John Kinzie dealt. Though the Indians were in and about Chicago in great numbers frequently, they did not have any permanent or important village there.

It has been but little more than one hundred years since the Potawatomi left Chicago for the west. The last great Indian dance was held in 1835. That was a great affair, a last expression of all the Indian felt about what he had suffered. He then went west and was soon forgotten by those who built their homes and carried on trade where once the Potawatomi hunted, camped and traded. Where only a few hundred Indians then roamed, millions of people now live in permanent homes. Instead of the war whoop there is now the shriek of hundreds of trains entering the city. Instead of the hunting and trapping of game there is now the greatest meat-packing business in the world. Instead of the wigwam or tepee there are the skyscrapers, great institutions and line homes. What was then a wilderness of trees and swamps with very few human beings is now a great wilderness of buildings of all kinds with a population numbering millions. All of this change has come about in a hundred years.

## Chapter Nine - Noted Potawatomi Chiefs

While the Potawatomi did not produce chiefs as famous as some Indian tribes, there are a number who deserve special attention and should be familiar names to the student of Indian history.

### To-pe-ne-bee

For more than forty years Topenebee was chief of the Potawatomi Indians. We do not know much about his life except in connection with his work as chief of his people. He was born at his father's village on the St. Joseph about the middle of the eighteenth century. His father, Anaquiba, was a noted chief in his day. Besides Topenebee, there was another son, Sawawk, whose daughter became the wife of the second chief, Pokagon. Anaquiba also had a daughter, Kaukeama, who became the wife of William Burnett.

We do not know when Topenebee succeeded his father as chief. We first find him as the first of the Potawatomi to sign the Treaty of Greenville in 1795. The secretary who wrote out his name spelled it Thu-pe-nebu. In the next twenty-five years he signed a number of treaties, always at the head of the list of chiefs. This fact indicates his popularity among all the Potawatomi, for they were well represented at all treaties and their leading chiefs were present.

There is some question as to when Chief Topenebee died. In various treaties the name Topenebee appears as head of the chiefs until 1833. However, Isaac McCoy, who lived near the old chief, said that he died as the result of a fall from his horse while he was drunk. (See McCoy's *Indian Missions,* p. 286.) Since McCoy is considered quite authentic and since he lived quite near To-penebee, we must take his statement as correct. The explanation is made that the son of the chief, also called Topenebee, was made chief in his father's place.

Cecilia Bain Buechner, in her splendid paper on the Pokagons, quotes the report of McCoy. She also quotes from Father Badin to Bishop Fenwick: "On the ninth of last June, 1832, a man named Topinebee, about twenty-five years of age, chief of the whole Poutouatamy nation, in a drunken fit killed Nanako, a man justly esteemed." The report goes on to say how the young Topenebee was condemned to death but was saved by the plea of an aged woman and by young Topenebee paying a good price to the family of the. murdered man. This report makes it quite clear that this young son of Topenebee had succeeded his father as chief.

No doubt Topenebee was a strong man in his earlier years and did much for his people. But he became much addicted to drink and lost his power and finer qualities. He signed his last treaty at Chicago, August 29, 1821. Here his good friend, Lewis Cass, tried to give him some advice. The reply that Topenebee is said to have made was this: "Father, we do not care for the land, nor the money, nor the goods. What we want is whisky. Give us whisky."

Topenebee was well known to many of the leading white men of the day. He gave a hearty welcome to Isaac McCoy when the latter came to the St. Joseph country to establish his mission. McCoy invited Topenebee and another chief, Chesbass, to dinner on January 1, 1823. At that time Topenebee had his settlement on the north side of the river but moved to the south side near the McCoy mission, about three miles southwest of the present Niles, Michigan. He was friendly to the McCoy mission and no doubt would have received and given much help for his people, but the awful curse of drink prevented him from being useful.

Topenebee was connected by marriage to many Indian and white families of the St. Joseph Valley. His sister, Kaukeama, was the wife of the trader, William Burnett. His daughter, Madeline, was the wife of the trader, Joseph Bertrand. Another daughter was one of the wives of the war chief, Wesau. His niece was the wife of the second chief, Leopold Pokagon.

Like most of the Potawatomi, Topenebee joined Tecumseh. However, we do not have record of much fighting against the Americans. Perhaps he was kept at peace by the influence of the good Potawatomi chief, Leopold Pokagon. Topenebee was present at the Fort Dearborn massacre and helped the Americans all he could. No doubt he would have been more widely and favorably known had he not fallen a victim to drink.

## Metea

Near the present town of Cedarville, on the St. Joseph River of the Maumee, seven miles northeast of Fort Wayne, Metea, one of the best known of the Potawatomi chiefs, had his village. From this place he went forth to many a battle and later to many treaty assemblies. He is said to have had an active part in the massacre of Fort Dearborn. He led the Indians in the attacks on Fort Wayne shortly afterwards. Here he was wounded severely. He was in advance of his men when suddenly he came upon a part of Harrison's army. He jumped behind a small tree but his elbow was exposed. Major Mann of Harrison's army fired and broke his arm. Metea rushed back through the forest towards his men, carrying his broken arm and hotly pursued by Major Mann and others. His arm never healed, and after the wars he often told of his encounter with the white man.

Metea attended important conferences with the Americans and signed the treaties at the Rapids of the Miami (Maumee) near Toledo, September 29, 1817; at St. Marys, Ohio, October 2, 1818; at Chicago, August 29, 1821; and at Paradise Springs (at Wabash), October 16, 1826. In these conferences he distinguished himself both as an orator and as a diplomat. He was respected by the Americans and had much influence with the Indians.

He was a full-blooded Potawatomi with marked Indian characteristics. He was six feet tall and dignified in bearing. He appeared sullen and obstinate.

His many experiences in bloody battles had left their impression. He usually had one eye painted red, significant of his savage nature. He often visited Detroit and Ft. Maiden to receive presents from the British,

**Chief Metea -** *Courtesy J. Fred Bippus*

whom he admired. He was interested in his people and later in life advocated and aided their education. But like too many of his people he fell a victim of drink. He attended a council with the Americans at Fort Wayne in 1827. Here he showed all his former dignity and ability. After the council he drank heavily, during which he drank some poison as well as whisky. Whether he did this by mistake or whether an opponent gave it to him has not been decided. He died the same day and was buried near the St. Mary's River in the western part of the present city of Fort Wayne.

Stephen H. Long describes Metea when he came to have a conference with General Tipton at Fort Wayne: "The name of this man was Metea, which signifies in the Potawatomi language, 'Kiss me.' He was represented to us as being the greatest chief of the nation; we had, however, an opportunity of ascertaining afterwards that he was not the principal chief, but that he had, by his talents as a warrior and his eloquence as an orator, obtained considerable influence in the councils of his nation. He may be considered as a partisan, who, by his military achievements, has secured to himself the command of an independent tribe. He resides on the St. Joseph, about nine miles from Fort Wayne, at the Indian village called Muskwawasepeotan, 'the town of the old red wood creek.' Being a chief of distinction, he came accompanied by his brother, as his rank required that he should be assisted by some one to light his pipe, and perform such other duties as always devolve upon attendants. Metea appears to be a man of about forty or forty-five years of age. He is a full-blooded Potawatomi; his stature is about six feet; he has a forbidding aspect, by no means deficient in dignity. His features are strongly marked, and expressive of a haughty and tyrannical disposition; his complexion is dark. Like most of the Potawatomi whom we met, he is characterized by a low, aquiline, and well-shaped nose. His eyes are small, elongated, and black; they are not set widely apart. His forehead is low and receding; the facial angle amounts to about eighty. His hair is black, and indicates a slight tendency to curl. His cheek bones are remarkably high and prominent, even for those of an Indian; they are not, however, angular, but present very distinctly the rounded appearance which distinguishes the aboriginal American from the

Asiatic. His mouth is large, the upper lip prominent. There is something unpleasant in his looks, owing to his opening one of his eyes wider than the other, and to a scar which he has upon the wing of his nostril. On first inspection his countenance would be considered as expressive of defiance and impetuous daring, but upon closer scrutiny it is found rather to announce obstinate constancy of purpose and sullen fortitude. We behold in him all the characteristics of the Indian warrior to perfection." [1]

## Shabbona

Shabbona was of Ottawa blood, a grand-nephew of the great chief, Pontiac. He was born on the Maumee River, Ohio, but at an early age migrated to Illinois where he later mar-

**Chief Shabbona - Courtesy Chicago Historical Society**

ried a Potawatomi woman, the daughter of a Potawatomi chief, Spatke. Later he was elected chief of the Potawatomi and became one of their most admirable men. He established his village in what is now Dekalb County. When the Shawnee, Tecumseh, came west, he had a long conference with Shabbona. He later became an admirer of the great chief and followed him to war against the Americans. When Tecumseh fell at the Battle of the Thames in 1814, Shabbona was at his side. After this battle he became disgusted with the way the British were using the Indians. He joined the American cause and was ever their trusted friend.

In 1827 during the Winnebago rebellion, Shabbona visited the Winnebago chief, Big Foot, on Lake Geneva, Wisconsin, and tried to persuade him from attacking the Americans. Big Foot took him prisoner and for a time threatened his life. He was released, but the Indians reproached him by calling him the White Man's Friend. During the Black Hawk war, Shabbona constantly warned the Americans about the intentions of the Indians. He saved many lives but gained the hatred of his race, for which he paid dearly in later years. One group of white people on Indian Creek, LaSalle County, Illinois, did not heed his warning and all were killed by the Indians. There today, fourteen miles north of Morris, is Shabbona Park, in honor of the Indian who was indeed the white man's friend.

In 1837 when the Potawatomi Indians were moved to western Iowa, near Council Bluffs, Shabbona went with his people to help them as best he could. While here some of his old enemies tried to kill him. He escaped them, but they did kill his son and nephew. He returned to his old home, now known as Shabbona Grove, near Shabbona, Illinois, where he lived until 1849.

He then moved to the new reservation for the Potawatomi in northern Kansas. After living with his people there for three years he returned to DeKalb County, Illinois, to find that the white men had taken possession of the two sections of land reserved for him in the Treaty of 1829. However, some white friends raised money to purchase him a home on the Illinois River, near Seneca. He was also given a small pension by the government for his services in the Black Hawk war. He died in 1859, and was buried in the city cemetery at Morris, Illinois. A large boulder marks his grave. He should be remembered by the term of reproach given him by his enemies of his own race, "The White Man's Friend."

One evidence of the honesty and bigness of this chief was his defense of General Harrison's honor and bravery. When the campaign of 1840 was on, some of the political opponents of General W. H. Harrison had called him a coward. Shabbona and Sauganash, Billy Caldwell, were at that time living on the Potawatomi reservation near Council Bluffs, Iowa. They wrote the following letter which was printed in the Chicago Daily American, June 9, 1840:

48

Council Bluffs, 23d March, 1840.

"To General Harrison's Friends:

"The other day, several newspapers were brought to us; and, peeping over them, to our astonishment, we found the hero of the late war called a coward. This would have surprised the tall braves, Tecumseh, of the Shawnees, and Round Head and Walk-in-the-Water of the Wyandotts. If the departed could rise again, they would say to the white men that General Harrison was the terror of the late tomahawkers. The first time we got acquainted with General Harrison, it was at the Council Fire of the late old Tempest, General Wayne, on the headwaters of the Wabash, at Greenville, 1795, from that time until 1811, we had many friendly smokes with him; but from 1812 we changed our tobacco smoke into powder smoke. Then we found General Harrison was a brave warrior, and humane to his prisoners, as reported to us by two of Tecumseh's young men who were taken in the fleet with Capt. Barcley on the 10th of September, 181 3; and on the Thames, where he routed both the red men and the British; and where he showed his courage, and his humanity to his prisoners, both white and red. We are the only two surviving of that day in this country. We hope the good white men will protect the name of General Harrison.

We remain your friends forever,

Shaub-e-nee, Aid to Tecumseh.
B. Caldwell, Captain.

## Winamac

There has been much misunderstanding about Chief Winamac, because there were two Potawatomi chiefs by the same name. One was friendly to the United States; the other was bitterly opposed to the Americans. The latter was killed in 1812 in a fight with the friendly Shawnee chief, Captain James Logan. The subject of this sketch died in 1821. His village was on the Wabash River, eleven miles downstream from the mouth of Eel River, where Logansport now stands.

While General Harrison was governor of Indiana territory, Winamac was his friendly aid in getting the Indians to make adjustments of their lands. Harrison wrote that Winamac was "an open and avowed friend of the United States." He was strongly opposed to Tecumseh. For this reason he was marked for death by the Shawnees. At one time in council, Tecumseh poured out a torrent of abuse upon Winamac and threatened his life. Winamac coolly got his pistol ready and was undisturbed by the threats of the great Shawnee chief. Tecumseh accused Winamac of trying to persuade the Indians to sell their lands to the United States. Winamac reported all the plans of Tecumseh to General Harrison. At one time he attended a great council held at Pare aux Vaches, now known as Bertrand, Michigan. There the council under Tecumseh's suggestions planned to kill all the old chiefs and enlist the younger ones against Harrison. Winamac continued to attend the Indian councils and at one time boldly told The Prophet that he lied. He must have had great influence to be so daring without being killed.

49

By some it was reported that he was one of the Indian leaders in the Battle of Tippecanoe. Other Indians said that he was not. Here again he probably was mistaken for the other Winamac who was strongly against the Americans at this time. The next year both of them were present at the massacre at Fort Dearborn. The unfriendly Winamac was one of the leaders. The friendly Winamac brought a message from General Hull of Detroit to Captain Heald and warned the captain not to trust the promises of the other Potawatomi chiefs.

Winamac signed the treaties at Fort Wayne in 1803 and 1809. After the war he signed the treaty of peace at the Rapids of the Maumee, and the Treaty of Paradise Springs in 1826. After his death, his village on the Wabash was included in a tract of land given to Abraham Burnett. His name is perpetuated in the city of Winamac, county seat of Pulaski County, Indiana.

## Sauganash, or Billy Caldwell

Sauganash, more familiarly known as Billy Caldwell, was the son of an Irish officer, Colonel Caldwell, in British service. His mother was a Potawatomi, remarkable for her beauty and wisdom. He was born in Canada about 1780, and was well educated in the Jesuit schools of Detroit. He was given the Indian name of Sauganash, meaning "The Englishman." Pie fought with the British against the Americans, and is said to have been with Tecumseh when he fell fighting the Americans in the Battle of Thames.

He was in the neighborhood of Fort Dearborn when the massacre occurred there August 15, 1812. After so many had been killed, some of the friendly Indians were trying to protect their old friends, members of the Kinzie family. Among these were the Potawatomi chiefs, Waubunsee and Black Partridge. At one time it looked as though their efforts would be entirely unsuccessful, and that all white prisoners would be massacred. Just then another Indian chief arrived. The unfriendly Indians asked him his name. "I am the Sau-ga-nash," came the reply. It was the Indian chief, Billy Caldwell, who aimed to say that he was the white man's friend. He entered the house, put his rifle behind the door as suspecting nothing, and then addressed the Potawatomi who had recently come with unfriendly attitudes:

"I was told there were enemies here, but I am glad to find only friends. Why have you blackened your faces? Is it because you are mourning for friends you have lost in the battle? Or is it that you are fasting? If so, ask your friend here and he will give you food. He is the Indians' friend and never yet refused them what they needed." The Indians were taken by surprise and were ashamed to state their real purpose. After receiving some presents they went away. The Kinzie family remained in hiding for some time and then were taken to the St. Joseph (Michigan) Potawatomi by To-pe-ne-bee.

Caldwell was with Tecumseh and the British in the War of 1812. About 1820 he left the service of the British for service with the Americans at Chicago. He went to the Winnebagoes in their rebellion of 1827 and tried to dissuade them from attacking the Americans. He influenced his people not to join Black Hawk in his war. In the treaty of Prairie du Chien he received two and one-half sections of land. In the treaty of Chicago, September 26, 1853, he received $5,000 cash and an annuity of $400 per year for life, while his children received $600. He was honorable, high-minded, and generous. In early Chicago he was justice of the peace, a regular voter, and had property.

In 1835 he joined the Potawatomi in their march to their new home in Iowa. He died on the Potawatomi reservation near Council Bluffs, September 28, 1841.

## Alexander Robinson

Alexander Robinson, whose Indian name was Cheche-bing-way, meaning blinking eyes, was the son of a Scotch trader and an Ottawa woman. He was born at Mackinaw, Michigan, in 1789. In 1794, though only five years old, he was present at the Battle of Fallen Timbers when General Anthony Wayne defeated the combined forces of many Indian tribes. Later he came west and identified himself with the Potawatomi. He came to be an influential chief among them. He was present at the massacre of Fort Dearborn and tried to keep the Indians from committing so much cruelty. He helped to rescue Captain Heald and wife by taking them in a canoe the entire length of Lake Michigan to Mackinaw. In later years he helped Chief Shabbona to keep the Potawatomi from joining Black Hawk in his rebellion.

In 1825 he married a woman three-fourths Indian. He was always more of a hunter and trader than a warrior. He spent much time in the Calumet region and for a time was in the employ of John Jacob Astor. He served as an interpreter between the whites and the Indians in some of their conferences. He signed the Treaty of Prairie du Chien, Wisconsin, July 29, 1829. Here he received two sections of land. In a treaty made at Chicago, September 26, 1833, he and Billy Caldwell received $5,000 each and an annuity for life, while each of their children received a small amount.

## Zachariah Cicott

One of the many traders along the Wabash River was a French Canadian by the name of Cicott. He married a Potawatomi squaw at what is now Independence, near Attica, Indiana. He and his Indian wife had five children. The oldest was named Zachariah.

When Zachariah was twelve years old he was sent to the Catholic school at Vincennes where he remained three years. During this time he made one or more trips to New Orleans. His father died when he was young. As the oldest of the family, he had the responsibility of helping his mother raise the family. He became skillful in all the ways and arts of the Indians of those days and at the same time he knew the white men also. He became a trader and also raised horses for sale.

When Tecumseh came west seeking allies among the Potawatomi, Zachariah opposed him, saying he was nothing more than an agent for the British. He became friendly to Harrison and became his trusted adviser. For all this his Indian friends became bitter towards him. He left Independence and went to Vincennes. From here he spent a year among the Indians of the south and did much to prevent their joining Tecumseh when this Shawnee chief went south in 1811 to win their support. He was a scout for General Harrison at Tippecanoe and during the War of 1812. At the close of the war he returned to Independence where he lived most of his life.

He married Elizabeth, daughter of the Potawatomi chief, Perig. By her he had three children, Jean Baptista, Emilia and Sophia. He increased his trade on the Wabash and became well-to-do. Because of his friendship for the Americans, the Potawatomi refused to elect him their chief, but instead gave this position of honor to his younger brother, George Cicott. As chief of the Potawatomi, George Cicott received three and one-half sections of land at the Treaty of Paradise Springs in 1826. (Lake Cicott is named for Chief George Cicott.) At the same treaty, Zachariah received one section while his son received the section of land that had been given to his grandfather, Chief Perig. His daughter, Emilia, was well educated and served as an interpreter at some of the treaties.

Zachariah Cicott was a fine looking man, more than six feet tall. He was swarthy, with keen, black eyes. He was a shrewd trader and became quite wealthy for his time. He died in 1850 and is buried beside his wife in the old cemetery just north of Independence on the old Potawatomi Trail and near the great Potawatomi Springs. His important and faithful services for the Americans have been overlooked by many Indiana history writers.

[1] Indian Tribes, by McKenney and Hall, Volume II, page 208.

# Chapter Ten - Some Famous Indian Traders

During the Indian and pioneer days there were many white men who were Indian traders. Most of them were here and there and for a short time only. They were traders only for what they could get out of it. Many of them married Indian squaws with no intention of living with them very long. Others who took Indian wives built up good homes, and their wives made good mothers and housekeepers. Some of these men became real pioneers and contributed much to the permanent welfare of the country. The following are a few of these men who had many dealings with the Potawatomi.

### William Burnett

The first permanent settler on the St. Joseph River in southwestern Michigan was William Burnett, who came from New Jersey about 1776. He spent one year in fur trading and then went to Mackinaw to sell his furs. Here he got in trouble with British agents who had him arrested and sent to Montreal. Later he returned to the St. Joseph to find all his property destroyed. He improved his position as an Indian trader by marrying Kaukeama, daughter of Anaquiba, and sister to the coming chief, Topenebee. The marriage of Burnett and Kaukeama occurred about 1782, with the Catholic priest officiating and with much pomp and ceremony.

While many of the marriages of fur traders with Indian women were only temporary and for some gain, William Burnett seems to have taken this marriage seriously. They built a good home about two miles from the mouth of the St. Joseph. Here Burnett planted an orchard which outlived its planter. To the Burnetts were born seven children: James, John, Abraham, Isaac, Jacob, Nancy and Rebecca. These children were all sent to school in Detroit.

During all these years Burnett was increasing his fur trade and his wealth. He had connection with the trading post on the site of Chicago and marketed his furs at Mackinaw. His wife too seems to have been a real princess of much financial ability. Since her husband was away most of the time she had to raise the children. Burnett himself was always friendly to the American cause. This caused him to get into trouble with the British and their sympathizers. He died about 1812 under circumstances not well known. Some think he might have been murdered by some of his opponents.

Nancy was married to John Davis of the Wabash country. Rebecca married and lived in Detroit. In the U. S. treaties with the Potawatomi the Burnett children received large grants of land. Little is known of any of the sons except Abraham. He became a bitter enemy to the United States. It is said that he planned an ambush of General Harrison's army while on its march to Tippecanoe. He took an active part in the battle. The creek that flows by the battle ground was named after him, Burnett's Creek. At the Treaty of Paradise Springs, 1826, Abraham Burnett was given three sections of land. One of these sections included the old village of Chief Winamac on the Wabash River, eleven miles down the river from Logansport. Here another creek was named after him while Burnettsville, White County, Indiana, also bears his name.

## Joseph Bertrand

Joseph Bertrand was one of the early pioneers and one of the most noted citizens of southwestern Michigan. Little is known of his early life. One report is that he was born in Canada and another that Mackinaw was his birthplace. It is said that he was a close relative of Henri Bertrand, friend and confidant of Napoleon Bonaparte.

Young Bertrand, like many a young Frenchman, came into the western wilderness seeking his fortune. It is likely that he was at first in the employ of William Burnett, who became his uncle by marriage. William Burnett married Kaukeama, sister to the main chief, Topenebee, and Joseph Bertrand married Madeline, daughter of Chief Topenebee. He established a trading post on the west side of the St. Joseph River about 1808. This was on the Great Sauk Trail and commanded much trade with the Indians. The site of this trading post is now covered by the St. Joseph River. Later he located on the bluff just opposite on the east side of the river.

At the Treaty in Chicago, August 29, 1821, Madeline Bertrand, wife of Joseph Bertrand, was given one section of land at the Pare aux Vaches (Parkavash) where his new location was. The meaning of this name was "cattle pens" for in an early day the buffalo came here in great numbers to feed on the grass growing on land that had been cleared by the Indians. Then, too, along the river were giant oaks which afforded much shade and shelter. It was a place of great beauty and well located.

**Bertrand, Michigan**
*Left* — **Where the Sauk Trail crossed the St. Joseph River. Where Joseph Bertrand had his trading post.**
*Right* — **Path leading to the old cemetery where the Catholic Mission and St. Mary's College began.**

Here Bertrand built up a successful trading post with stations in other places more or less distant. On the Great Sauk Trail Indians came in large numbers and brought their furs to trade for goods that Bertrand had for sale. This trail became the Detroit-Chicago road and so became a trading center for the early pioneer. Bertrand became a stopping place for travelers and a great pleasure resort. Many are the stories of the jolly days in and about the two taverns that were located there.

Bertrand became a great religious center as well, for Catholic missionaries as early as 1700 were there. When Joseph Bertrand located here these early missions were revived. The early chapel was replaced in 1836 by a brick church, the first church house in southwestern Michigan. Here the Catholic sisters started a school for girls. This later was moved across the line into Indiana and was the beginning of the famous St. Mary's College. In all of this Joseph Bertrand took an active part.

When he located at Pare aux Vaches he built a new house, but it is said that his Indian wife, Madeline, preferred to spend most of her time in a tepee in the back yard. To the Bertrands were born a number of children. At the Treaty of Chicago when she received a section of land, each of her children received a half-section at the Kankakee portage near South Bend. Their names are given as Joseph, Benjamin, Lawrence, Theresa, and Amable. In the Treaty of 1826 two more of her children were given a half-section each. They are named as Luke and Julia, and were likely born between 1821 and 1826. At the treaty made at the Carey Mission, September 20, 1828, Madeline was given one section of land and each of her children one-half section. At the Chicago treaty, September 26, 1833, Madeline and each of her seven children were given $250 each. Three other Bertrands were mentioned: Joseph H., Mary, and M. L. However, it is likely that the last three were of another Bertrand family. On August 10, 1837, eighteen Potawatomi chiefs acknowledged their indebtedness to Joseph Bertrand for $5,229.03, and asked the United States to make payment out of their annuities.

So Joseph Bertrand was a prominent man. By marriage he was related to the most prominent Potawatomi. By trade and business he was acquainted with some of the leading men of his day. He was a friend of Isaac McCoy who established the Carey Mission west of Niles. He often met Lewis Cass, Michigan's noted statesman. Over the Chicago-Detroit road the leading men of the country passed in their travel between these two cities. Bertrand was a favorite stopping place and a great center of trade until Niles on the north and South Bend on the south took away its trade.

The Indian name of his wife was Mona. When she was baptized she was christened Madeline. With Bertrand this was a real marriage and for life. She died in 1847, and her tombstone may still be seen in the old churchyard on the north side of Bertrand. There also stood the brick church which ministered to the spiritual needs of both whites and Indians for many years. On the stone are engraved these words, "Ellen, wife of Joseph Bertrand." Her daughter, Julia, in later years said that the engraver just misunderstood her name.

Just what became of the Bertrand fortune is not known. It is likely that he had financial reverses. His children went west to the Potawatomi reserve in Kansas. He followed about 1858. He died in 1862 and is buried at St. Mary's, Kansas.

## Joseph Bailly

Joseph Bailly is one of the few men who have left their names on the map of north-western Indiana. He was the son of Michael Bailly, an aristocratic Frenchman of Montreal. After his father's death, Joseph came west to seek his fortune. In 1795, at the age of twenty-one, he was a trader among the Indians of Michigan territory. He married the daughter of an Indian chief and became prominent as a trader among the Indians. By his first marriage he had five sons and one daughter: Alexis, Joseph, Michael, Philip, Francis and Sophie. He separated from his first wife and in 1810 married the divorced widow of a Frenchman, herself of French-Indian blood. By this marriage he had four daughters and one son: Esther, Rose, Helen, Hortense and Robert. During these early years of the century he was increasing in wealth as well as in the size of his family.

In 1822 he moved his family to the Calumet region, among the Potawatomi. He located on the north bank of the Little Calumet River not far from the present site of Chesterton. The land was one wild wilderness. The Bailly family was the only one of white blood in north-western Indiana. He received his mail from Fort Dearborn. He was on the main trail from Fort Dearborn to Detroit. He was a long-distance from the Bertrand trading post and the Carey Mission in southern Michigan. Here in this great wilderness he lived and prospered. He purchased furs from his Potawatomi neighbors. He marketed his goods at Mackinaw, transporting the cargoes by rafts on Lake Michigan. He had trading posts as far away as Baton Rouge, Louisiana, and Montreal, Canada. From these places he brought back many things to sell to the Indians.

Joseph Bailly was more than a mere trader. He took a great interest in educating his children. He sent his daughters to Fort Wayne and Detroit for their education. He sent his son, Robert, to the Baptist mission conducted by Isaac McCoy near Niles, Mich. Here Robert died in 1827 of typhoid fever. Though Bailly was a Catholic, he and McCoy were great friends. Bailly had many friends and his home became a stopping place for many prominent travelers. He had a fine home for the wilderness and other good buildings for his employees. He had a good library for that day and many other things to make his home pleasant. His children married into some of the most prominent families of that day. Through their mothers they were of Potawatomi blood. In the treaty with the Potawatomi at Chicago in 1833 they received grants amounting to fifteen hundred dollars.

Joseph Bailly laid out a town to be known as Bailly. He gave names to the streets after his daughters. He died in 1835 before this village could be built, but another Bailly town was erected nearer the lake. U. S. Route 12 passes through this village. North of it is the Bailly cemetery where Joseph Bailly and his family lie buried. One mile to the east is still to be seen the old Bailly homestead with some of the original buildings preserved.

## John Kinzie

One of the best-known white men who had much to do with the Indians was John Kinzie, who built the first real residence in Chicago. His father's name was McKenzie, but John later dropped the prefix. He was born in Quebec, December 27, 1763. After his father's death his mother married Wm. Forsyth. To this marriage were born five sons, half-brothers to John Kinzie.

Later records indicate many dealings with his half-brothers. John Kinzie first married Margaret McKenzie, who had spent years of her youth as a captive among the Indians. By her he had three children. While the Kinzie family were living in Detroit, Mrs. Kinzie's father came in search of his lost daughter. She took her children and returned with her father to Virginia. Her husband offered little objection. Later he married Eleanor (Little) McKillip, the widow of a British officer killed in the Battle of Fallen Timbers. She had three children by her first husband.

Before his last marriage, John Kinzie had spent some years as a trader at Fort Wayne and along the Maumee. At that time he was a British sympathizer and left the Maumee Valley on the approach of Wayne's army. He then located as a trader on the St. Joseph River at Bertrand, Michigan. To this place he brought his wife and family in 1798 and remained six years. In the meantime he had extended his trading posts to the site of the new fort just built on the southwest shore of Lake Michigan and named Fort Dearborn. To this place Kinzie brought his family in 1804. He purchased the cabin that had been erected by Pierre LeMai just across the Chicago River from Fort Dearborn. He enlarged this into a home that became well known to the inhabitants of the fort. To this place the officers and their wives in the fort went for outings while canoes were always waiting at the riverside to convey the Kinzie family to the fort in case of an Indian attack.

John Kinzie prospered in business during these first years in Chicago. He was a silversmith and would make attractive articles which the Indians wanted and for which they exchanged their furs. Although Kinzie had some unfortunate quarrels with some of his white neighbors, he became a great friend of the Indians. When the Indians became threatening during the summer of 1812, they did not attack the Kinzie home. When the attack on Fort Dearborn was about to be made, the Kinzies were warned by the Indians. During and after the massacre, they were shielded and spared by the intervention of some of their Indian friends. They were taken around the lake, to the St. Joseph settlements and soon reached Detroit where they spent the next four years.

When Fort Dearborn was rebuilt in 1816, the Kinzies returned to their old home. John Kinzie had lost much and could not regain his business. His oldest son, James, by his first wife, came to Chicago and became prosperous. He gave his father much help during these years. His son, John H., a son by his second wife, also became prosperous. He married Juliette McGill who, as Mrs. John H. Kinzie, is widely known by her book, Waubun, the most complete early history of Chicago and the Northwest. Others of his children and brothers married into prominent families. The Kinzie home was widely known during the early years of Chicago.

John Kinzie did not recover from his loss at the time of the Chicago massacre. He died in January, 1828. On September 20, 1828, the United States made a treaty with the Potawatomi at the Carey Mission near Niles, Michigan. One paragraph of that treaty is of special interest:

"To Eleanor Kinzie and her four children by the late John Kinzie is given $3,500, in consideration of the Indians for her deceased husband who was long an Indian trader, and who lost a large sum in trade by credits given them and also by the destruction of property. The money is given in lieu of a tract of land which the Indians gave to the late John Kinzie long since and upon which he lived."

## Gurdon S. Hubbard

The life of Gurdon S. Hubbard forms a connecting link in the history of Chicago extending over a period of almost seventy years. He was born in Windsor, Vermont, August 22, 1802. His father was a lawyer. He moved to Montreal, went into business and lost what money he had. The son, Gurdon, much against the wishes of his parents, engaged with the American Fur Trading Company for five years' service. First at Mackinaw, then down to the Illinois country, back and forth on fur-trading expeditions, young Hubbard gained a great knowledge of the pioneer west. He learned to know and like the Indians. He was brave and without fear in the moment of danger. He frequently had dangerous encounters with drunken and enraged Indians.

The superintendent of his company was a Mr. DesCamps. At one time young Hubbard spent several months at Lake Peoria, Illinois. Here he made trips to Indian centers where he met such chiefs as Black Hawk and Shabbona. One old chief, Waba, wanted to adopt him as his son and gave him the name of Che-mo-co-mon-ess, meaning the Little American. In other sections he became known by the name of Papa-ma-ta-be, meaning the swift walker. In his journeys through Chicago he would make the home of John Kinzie his stopping place. So at an early age he became identified with the interests of the future metropolis.

After five years of service for the American Fur Trading Company he was discharged with ninety dollars to his credit and with a great training and experience. He thought of returning to the east. About this time, however, Mr. DesCamps resigned as superintendent for the company, and Hubbard was offered the position at $1,300 a year. He held this place for two years and then purchased the interests of the company in Illinois. Instead of using only boats, Hubbard now employed pack horses to transport his goods across the portages. He extended the use of these pack horses in taking his goods far to the south to trading posts which he established. One of these extended as far south as Danville, one hundred twenty-five miles. This became known as Hubbard's Trace, and later became an Illinois state road which was taken over and improved by the state.

In connection with Mr. Hubbard there was a romance that has become historic. The old chief of the Kankakee Potawatomi, Tamin, took such a liking to Hubbard that he wanted the young trader to marry his daughter. Hubbard knew that the favor of this old chief was necessary to his success. But because the proposed bride was older than he and not very desirable, Hubbard proposed marriage with the niece of the old chief. Her name was Watseka. She was a favorite of her tribe, and had been chosen to perpetuate the memory of a former woman by that name who had helped the Potawatomi defeat their ancient enemies, the Iroquois. The old chief consented, but Watseka was only ten years old. Hubbard said he would wait till she was older, hoping that something would turn up that would make the marriage unnecessary. But when Watseka was about fifteen her mother brought her to Hubbard and insisted that the marriage contract be fulfilled. Hubbard and Watseka lived together for about two years. She bore him two daughters, both of whom died in infancy. Then Hubbard began to think of accepting the more civilized way of life. Watseka understood and so the couple separated. But in later years Hubbard always spoke of his Indian wife as attractive, generous and agreeable.

After her separation from Hubbard, Watseka married his successor in business, a Frenchman, Novel Lavasseur. She lived with him for ten years and bore him several children. Then with him she had the same experience as with Hubbard. With her children she went west with her people. Years afterwards she came back to Illinois to visit the scenes of her childhood and romances. The story of her life became well known. Today the city of Watseka, Illinois, perpetuates the memory of this beautiful Indian woman.

Hubbard became quite permanently identified with Chicago by the early thirties. He had trading posts on Hubbard's Trace as far south as Danville. During the Winnebago rebellion in 1827 he performed a brave act in riding to Danville to secure help for Chicago which was threatened by an attack of the enraged Indians. In a few days he returned to Chicago with a company of men to defend the city.

After the Black Hawk war in 1832, Chicago went on a boom. Hubbard made a neat little fortune by proper investments and sales at the right time. From then on until his death on September 14, 1886, he was one of the most active and respected of Chicago's citizens. He started the meat packing business for which Chicago has become so famous. He was Chicago's first banker. He organized the first fire department. He helped to organize the first Episcopalian church and was a faithful member. He was responsible for the location of the Illinois canal. He held various orifices in the city. He has been characterized as the last and the greatest of the pioneers. He had active associations with the Potawatomi of the early days of Fort Dearborn and lived to see Chicago one of the greatest cities of the nation.

**Isaac McCoy**　　　　**Christiana McCoy**
*Courtesy Indiana Historical Society*

# Chapter Eleven - Isaac McCoy

## Modern Apostle to the American Indians and Father of Indian Territory

"The Indian school of Isaac McCoy has often been mentioned by Indiana writers, but the significance of his work has been overlooked. McCoy was a most remarkable character. Many of the pioneer preachers underwent great hardships, but no other equalled McCoy in this respect. In fact, St. Paul himself had no more strenuous life."

This strong characterization of the subject of this sketch by Jacob Piatt Dunn, one of our best Indiana historians, should give us interest in the study of his life.

Isaac McCoy was born in Fayette County, Pennsylvania, June 13, 1784. His father was a Baptist preacher. When Isaac was six years old, the family moved to Kentucky. Here he grew to manhood, greatly influenced by a strong religious home life and by pioneer experiences. In 1802 he married Christiana Polke, daughter of Charles Polke, also a Baptist preacher. Mr. Polke later became a member of the Indiana State Constitutional Convention.

Isaac McCoy and his wife were interested in mission work from the first. For a time after their marriage they lived at Vincennes and then moved to Clarke County, Indiana, where his father had been pastor. Here he was licensed to preach. Again they moved near Vincennes where he became pastor of the Maria Creek Baptist church. He also did farming, made spinning wheels and repaired farming implements in general.

After the War of 1812, McCoy became very much interested in missions to the Indians. His Baptist brethren were not too much interested, but gave him an appointment as a missionary to the Indians. He had many difficulties to overcome. He had difficulty in learning the Indian language. Pioneers as well as the Indians were not interested in his proposed school. He began his work in 1819 with six white children and one Indian, but progress was slow and discouragements many. About this time he visited the Delaware Indians, who lived along White River. These Indians were about to be moved west of the Mississippi. The old chief, Captain Anderson, told McCoy that if they could find a home in the west where the white man would leave them in peace, then he might come and talk school to them.

McCoy now thought it would be well to open a mission school among the Miamis of the Mississinewa or at their central village, Fort Wayne. He received a friendly invitation from Fort Wayne to locate his school there. He made a long trip through the wilderness to see what might be done. On this trip he had opportunity to see the awful condition of the Indians due to drink. Dr. Turner, the Indian agent at Fort Wayne, very much insisted that the school should be located there rather than on the Mississinewa. McCoy accepted and prepared to move his family and school. The journey through the wilderness was long, dangerous, and tiresome. But the McCoys kept on courageously and began their work at the new station. From the very first Mrs. McCoy was as brave as her husband and was his constant associate in their work and in their suffering.

The McCoys opened school in Fort Wayne, in May, 1820, with ten English students, 6 French, 8 Indians and one Negro. Mrs. McCoy taught the girls domestic arts. He taught the boys mechanical arts. It was difficult for him to secure teachers to assist. There were no other white settlements in northern Indiana outside of the small village and fort at Fort Wayne.

McCoy was a pioneer in education as well as in missions to the Indians. He had many difficulties. The citizens were interested in little but trade with the Indians; and in this trading they brought upon the red man the terrible curse of drink. McCoy was soon convinced that he could do little permanent good for the Indian so long as he lived among the white men and practiced their vices.

However, the need for a mission school was great. McCoy received some help and encouragement from the Baptist church. Lewis Cass, governor of Michigan territory, saw the great need of the thing that McCoy was doing, and granted him some help. Some of the Indians showed interest and were received as members in the Baptist church. Among these were two daughters of the famous Indian scout, William Wells.

Bands of Potawatomi Indians would visit Fort Wayne for trading purposes. Among these was Chief Menominee of the Potawatomi band whose homes were in what is now Marshall County. On urgent invitation of Menominee, McCoy visited these Indians and was much impressed by their interest. They wanted him to locate among them. On this trip he also met the grand chief of the Potawatomi, Topenebee, whose village was near Niles, Michigan.

The treaty between the Potawatomi and the United States representatives in Chicago in 1821 gave much encouragement to McCoy. A section of land was given for a mission school one mile west of the St. Joseph River in Michigan, and the government gave a thousand dollars a year for a schoolteacher and a blacksmith. With the prospect of this help, McCoy went to Washington and Philadelphia where he received encouragement for his project both from government officials and from the Mission Board of the Baptist church. After much preparation, McCoy moved his family and the school from Ft. Wayne to the new station in December, 1823. It was a great undertaking to make this journey of one hundred miles through the wilderness in the dead of winter. They had to take with them hogs and cattle. With no roads save Indian trails, no bridges whatever across the streams, and with no houses for shelter along the way, the journey was quite hazardous.

On New Year's Day, 1823, McCoy entertained at his new station the head Potawatomi chief, Topenebee. For nearly fifty years this Indian had been the leader of his people. But he was now getting old and very much addicted to drink. However, it was good for McCoy to have the friendship of this influential Potawatomi. His village was not far away from the place of the Carey Mission.

On January 27, 1823, the McCoys opened their new school. It was called the "Carey Mission," named after the great missionary, William Carey. They had thirty Indian students. But their difficulties and handicaps were many. The winter was very cold. The hastily constructed school had no floor, door or chimney. A big fire was built on the ground in the center of the room. The smoke was annoying. They had to feed and house these Indian students. They had great difficulty in getting provisions. They sent back to Fort Wayne, a hundred miles away, for more provisions. In the meantime they had little to eat. An old Potawatomi squaw brought them a mess of sweet corn. Mr. Bertrand, the French trader, divided with them his supplies. By the middle of February supplies had arrived. McCoy was happy, though he had much sickness and often was near death.

This was the beginning of a most serious effort to educate and Christianize the Indians. Though McCoy was in poor health he would make trips on horseback to Ohio and to the east for support of the mission. In his absence Mrs. McCoy would direct the mission and do much of the work herself. They sent their sons to Columbian College in Washington in order that they might be prepared to help their parents in their great work.

Governor Lewis Cass of Michigan Territory was friendly to him. He sent commissioners to investigate the work. These made an excellent report in 1824. The governor was interested in literary, religious, and vocational training for these Indians. McCoy was somewhat of a genius as a mechanic and did all he could to teach the Indians the arts of agriculture and mechanics. He extended his visits to the Ottawa Indians who lived on Grand River, some seventy-five miles to the north. Here he met a friendly Ottawa chief, Noaqua Keshuck, or Noonday, who had his village on the Kalamazoo River. Noonday urged McCoy to open a school and a mission among the Ottawas. One of the speeches of this old Indian has been preserved:

"We are all rejoiced that you have come to live among us. You have told us to be good and I tell you that ever since you first talked to me about God, I have been trying to be good. And since that time I and a few others have often endeavored to persuade others to be good. For my own part I acknowledge that I know nothing correctly about the Great Spirit, and I am glad that you have come to live among us, and regularly preach to us about him." [1]

By the aid of the Baptist Board and assistance from the government, a mission and a school were established on Grand River near what is now the city of Grand Rapids. McCoy brought his family here for a time and personally directed the work among the Ottawas. It was known as the Thomas Mission. But he kept in very close touch with the work among the Potawatomi at the Carey Mission on the St. Joseph.

The Carey Mission grew rapidly. Many improvements were made on the farm. Much wheat and other grain and vegetables were raised. A mill was erected to grind wheat. It was the only mill within a hundred miles. The old Potawatomi chief, Topenebee, moved his village to the same side of the river as the mission, so as to be near his white friends. Some of the Indian students were sent east to school. Visitors and officials to the mission reported excellent progress. In the latter part of November, 1825, one Jotham Meeker joined the mission. He was to become a forceful character not only here but also in Kansas after the Indians were moved west.

As the mission grew, difficulties also grew. These were largely due to the coming of the white men. They had no interest in the Indians and wanted them out of the country. They sold the Indian whisky, which degraded and impoverished him. The old chief, Topenebee, became more and more a victim of drink. He would sell his last acre of ground for more whisky. While drunk, he fell from his horse and was killed July 26, 1826. The white men would often take advantage of the Indian and cheat him out of what little he had. McCoy became discouraged trying to help the Indians when so handicapped by the presence of white men. He began to think seriously of establishing a country beyond the Mississippi where he hoped they could develop an Indian civilization unspoiled by the vices of the white men.

In the fall of 1826, McCoy accompanied the Potawatomi to the treaty grounds of Paradise Springs, where the city of Wabash now stands. Many of his Indian students went with him. Here he received many favors from the United States commissioners in the treaty. He received the promise of two thousand dollars per year for twenty-two years for their education. Fifty-eight of his Indian students were given 160 acres of ground each to enable them to carry on their work of education. But at this treaty, McCoy was further impressed with his idea of moving the Indians to the west. For this project he began to receive the attention and interest of high officials at Washington.

McCoy was in Washington early in 1828. Here he made up his mind to explore the west to see what could be done. With but little money in sight he prepared for the trip. He took with him three Potawatomi and three Ottawa. Among the latter was his old friend, the Ottawa chief, Noonday. McCoy sent his family to their friends in Kentucky. He left the Carey and Thomas missions in the hands of others. With his Indian friends he proceeded by way of St. Louis to explore the lands of Kansas. They spent six weeks on this trip. McCoy selected Fayette, Missouri, as a place of residence for his family when they came west to work. When he returned to St. Louis his Potawatomi and Ottawa friends returned to Michigan, while he joined a party of Chickasaw and Choctaw Indians for a long visit and survey of the lands in what is now Oklahoma. On such trips as these he endured many hardships which were most severe on his weak constitution. He returned to his family on January 1, 1829, and soon left for Washington to make a full report of his western trips. Here he received much encouragement. Even President Jackson approved his plans and placed much of the direction in his hands.

From Washington, McCoy again visited the Carey and Thomas missions. Leaving the work in the hands of others, he moved his family to Fayette, Missouri. After another tour of Kansas lands he again went to Washington to influence authorities in favor of his idea of a western state for Indians. Returning to Fayette, he continued his western surveys. His sons, college graduates, joined their father in his mission, but they could not endure the strenuous work. One of them died early in 1830 and others of his children were soon taken. To be closer to his work, he moved his family from Fayette to the Shawnee mission, on the line between Missouri and Kansas, south of Kansas City. From here he was gone most of the time either making surveys of lands in Kansas or south in Indian Territory, or going on horseback to Washington to get support of his work.

It is almost impossible to realize the extent of the work of this great missionary without reading his own account of his activities and sufferings. It would seem almost impossible for any one person to do so much work. During his twenty years of service in the field, he made twelve trips to Washington and the east. Almost all of this was by horseback, accompanied by pioneer hardships. His many trips through the forests of Indiana and Michigan, and many more through the unsettled lands of Kansas and Indian Territory, seem almost incredible for one who was not strong physically. Again and again he was near unto death, but he would carry on.

Rev. and Mrs. McCoy were the parents of thirteen children. She was as brave and courageous as he, and was of a stronger physical constitution. Poor as they were and living here and there in the wilderness, they did not neglect the education of their children. They sent them to schools in the older white settlements. Two of their sons were educated as doctors and returned to the wilderness to help their parents. The children, however, could not so well endure this rigorous life. Ten of them died during the work here and there. The two doctors and two married daughters were among those to succumb.

Besides the arduous work, including the most menial and difficult physical labor, McCoy was a constant and voluminous writer. He was constantly writing about the Indians and about the best methods of dealing with them. A full collection of his works has been compiled in more than thirty volumes, now on file in the Kansas State Library. His own autobiography may be found in his book published in 1840, entitled "Baptist Indian Missions." It is much more than a book on denominational activities. It is first-hand information about pioneer conditions in dealing with the Indians of the Northwest Territory and in the west. Besides his own writings, information about his work may be had from hundreds of other books and pamphlets dealing with the history of these places.

Isaac McCoy has been called the Father of Indian Territory. While others from selfish motives were anxious to get rid of the Indians in the east, he was advocating their removal to the west so that they might be free from the vices of the white men. He would give them a new home where they could have a state of their own governed more to their nature and needs. In securing the organization of Indian Territory for the Indians he thought his great aim had been accomplished. But alas! he could hardly foresee that even here the Indian would not be beyond the greed and cruelty of the white man. He could not look forward a hundred years and see the Oklahoma of today where the Indian has met much the same fate that he had formerly met back east.

While McCoy had received much help from the government, he saw that other agencies must help. In 1842 he organized the American Indian Mission Association. He located at Louisville, Kentucky, to take charge of this work. Here he died July 21, 1846, at the age of sixty-two. Besides the faithful help of his wife and children, his niece, Eliza McCoy, gave her life to the same work. She was one of the most noted of Indian missionaries. In her own right she was well-to-do and left her fortune to carry on the work.

On McCoy's monument in the old Western Cemetery at Louisville are inscribed these words: "For nearly thirty years his entire time and energies were devoted to the civil and religious improvement of the aboriginal tribes of this country. He projected and founded the plan for their own colonization, their only hope, and the imperishable monument of his wisdom and benevolence." [2]

[1] Baptist Mission, p. 298.          [2] Indiana and Indianans, J. P. Dunn, p. 361.

# Chapter Twelve - The Pokagons

$A$mong the most desirable and admirable of the Potawatomi chiefs are the two Pokagons, father and son. Leopold and Simon. The lives of these two men form a connecting link between the days of the American pioneers to the present time; from the days of savagery to the days of modern civilization.

Leopold Pokagon is said to have been the son of a Chippewa father and an Ottawa mother. He was born about 1775 somewhere in Michigan. He was captured by a Potawatomi chief and presented to Chief Topenebee of the Potawatomi. Topenebee liked the young man and called him Pokagon because he was wearing as a part of his head gear a rib of a slain Potawatomi enemy. The word Pokagon means rib. Because Pokagon was brave and courageous Topenebee gave to him for a wife the daughter of Sawawk, the chief's brother. Here we have an interesting combination of the three closely related tribes — the son of a Chippewa father and an Ottawa mother marrying a Potawatomi woman.

We know very little of his early life except that it was likely the usual round of activities common to the American Indian. At that time he liked to fight as most Indians did. It is thought that he might have gone on one of those long journeys through the wilderness beyond the Mississippi to make war on the Osages, for in later years when he contrived a kind of two-wheeled wagon, he took as his pattern the kind of two-wheeled cart that might have been seen in the southwest.

***Upper* — Site of Carey Mission, one mile west of Niles, Michigan.**
***Lower* — Site of Pokagon Chapel, two miles west of Bertrand.**

Pokagon was not at the massacre of Fort Dearborn. He and his father-in-law, Sawawk, were in northern Michigan. Hearing about the prospective battle, they rode in haste but did not arrive until after the battle and massacre. They helped Topenebee and others care for the survivors, some of whom were taken to their St. Joseph country.

When Isaac McCoy first settled among the Potawatomi of the St. Joseph he soon became acquainted with Pokagon. McCoy has given us some interesting things about this chief. His village was a few miles south of the Carey Mission. It was on or near the old Sauk Trail, about two miles southwest of the trading post, Bertrand, on the St. Joseph. There today may be seen the spring and Pokagon Creek where once stood the village and the chapel.

While Pokagon was friendly to McCoy, he could not accept the Protestant form of religion. At an early day, even back in the seventeenth century, Catholic missionaries had come among these Indians. The ministry of these missionaries had continued off and on through the years. Pokagon had come in touch with their influence. He had made long journeys to take part in the Catholic church service. The coming of McCoy made the semi-Christian chief anxious for the Catholic missionaries to return. He told McCoy that he preferred the "black robes." In 1830 Father John Frederick Reze was sent to them. He could not remain long, so Pokagon went to Detroit to secure another priest. He appealed to the church officials in Detroit in the following words as quoted by Cecilia Bain Buechner:

"Father, I come to beg you to give us a Black-gown to teach us the word of God. We are ready to give up whisky and all our barbarous customs. Thou dost not send us a Black-gown and thou hast often promised us one. What, must we live and die in our ignorance? If thou hast no pity on us men, take pity on our poor children who will live as we have lived, in ignorance and vice. We are left deaf and blind, steeped in ignorance, although we earnestly desire to be instructed in the faith. Father, draw us from the fire, the fire of the wicked manitou. The American minister (McCoy) wished to draw us to his religion, but neither I nor any of the village would send our children to his school, nor go to his meetings. We have preserved the way of prayer taught our ancestors by the Blackgown who used to be at St. Joseph. Every night and morning my wife and children pray before a crucifix which thou hast given us, and on Sunday we pray oftener." One reason why Pokagon and other Indians preferred Catholic services was that the Indians could not read and so could not take part in Protestant services. They could be interested in the form of Catholic service.

In response to the plea of Pokagon, Father Badin was sent to them. The memory of the work of former priests was still effective and it was not long before many of the Indians were baptized. Pokagon had a rude chapel erected and over the front entrance there was a room for the priest, who had to use a ladder to reach his humble living room. This was the first church erected in this part of the country. Good work seems to have been done, for in 1835 the report showed that 650 Indians had been baptized.

Pokagon assisted the priests in every way he could. At certain hours all of his people must assemble for prayers and the service of the mass. The chief saw the awful effects of liquor among the Indians. He did not drink himself, and would keep his people from drink. In this he had a difficult time as soon as the white men came to tempt his Indians. He was honest and upright and insisted upon his people living that way. He was stern and courageous, but was sympathetic for an Indian, and often showed kindness to others. Not only the priests but other visitors to Pokagon's village bear evidence of the piety and sincerity in worship. It was a worship that calmed the savage breast and lifted him to a better plain of living. Often their piety was in great contrast to the rough ways of the pioneer.

Pokagon attempted to improve his village and his farms by better buildings and fences. At first he tried to employ some white settlers. They were taking advantage of him when Isaac McCoy and his workers from the Carey Mission helped him out. They built for him three log cabins, fenced twenty acres of ground, and helped them get started in raising cattle. Pokagon had his cabin along the creek, near the chapel. The other cabins and wigwams were not far away. The squaws raised corn in the fields down the creek and near the St. Joseph River.

Many of the pioneers around South Bend and along the St. Joseph have left statements of their visits to the Pokagon village. While the cabins and wigwams were rude and simple, there was evidence of an attempt to rise above the condition of their savage ancestors. The priests who had been educated in France or in the older sections of America endured and sacrificed much to live with, and serve, these primitive people.

Pokagon had many prominent visitors come to his village, but perhaps no one was more so than Johnny Appleseed. This famous, but odd, character had his last home near Fort Wayne, but he had roamed over Ohio, Indiana, and elsewhere planting apple seeds, that the coming generation might have plenty of apples. Tall, barefooted, and with a broad brimmed hat, Johnny Appleseed presented a unique appearance. Tn his rounds he came to the Pokagon village. The old chief received him kindly and when Johnny Appleseed expressed his desire to go south to the Tippecanoe country in Indiana, Pokagon took him in his own wagon. It must have been an unusual scene to see these two men of such odd appearance riding on a high seat of a brilliantly painted, two-wheeled wagon of unusual make and drawn by an ox and a horse.

Pokagon knew not only the most prominent Indians of his day, but also many prominent white men. He was present and took part in the treaties at the Carey Mission in 1828 and at Chicago in 1833, in which some of the leading Americans took part. He and Chief Menominee made a trip east to Philadelphia and other cities. He knew the great traders of the day, William Burnett, Joseph Bertrand, John Kinzie, and others. He knew Black Hawk who af-

terwards led his warlike Indians over the Sauk Trail to Detroit. By his eloquence Pokagon kept his Indians from joining Black Hawk in the war of
1832.

Pokagon was second chief of the St. Joseph Potawatomi, while his uncle,
Topenebee, was first chief, not only of the St. Joseph Potawatomi but of the
entire tribe. He saw the land that had been granted to him and his tribe
gradually taken over by the whites. His tribe had owned all of southwestern
Michigan and the land where Chicago now stands. He attended the great
gathering held at the Carey Mission in 1828 and signed the treaty whereby
the Potawatomi ceded to the United States the southwestern corner of Michigan. At the treaty made on the Tippecanoe in 1832 he and his wife each received a section of land, while his tribe received some forty-nine sections
along the St. Joseph. The next year, however, at Chicago, he was forced to
sign the treaty that ceded to the United States all of the land that had belonged to his tribe for generations.

Pokagon did receive in this treaty $2,000 instead of any further reserva-
tion. With this money and with the money received from the sale of the two
sections granted him and his wife in 1832, he began looking for a new location. He had three years to vacate the lands where his village had stood. He
had been granted permission to remain in the east with his family, and to
receive their annuities here. He purchased a tract of land of some seven hundred acres in the northern part of Cass County, Michigan, around what was
known as Long Lake, about four miles northwest of Dowagiac.

He moved his own family and that of his immediate tribe to this new home
in 1837. One of the first things done in this place was the building of a Catholic church. Notwithstanding all that he had suffered, he did not lose his faith.
The chapel was small but was the beginning of the Silver Creek Catholic,
church today, a beautiful brick structure on the land formerly owned by
Chief Leopold Pokagon.

During the few years left to him in his new home, he did all he could for his
people. His band lived together on the new land acquired and did not divide
it for individual ownership. This proved to be embarrassing to the Indians
after his death. Though of rugged constitution, Pokagon could not endure the
long list of wrongs that had been committed against him. The loss of his old
home and the lands connected with it, the loss of his many friends who had
been forced into exile, the loss of faith in the good intentions of the white
men were too much for him. He died July 8, 1841, in his sixty-sixth year. He
had been chief of his people for forty-two years. He was buried by the church
which he loved so well. His wife lived ten years longer. Their graves are now
beneath the new church which is a fitting monument for one who, though
born in almost a savage state, accepted the Christian religion and became a
faithful follower of the Nazarene.

After the death of Leopold Pokagon, his oldest sons, Paul and Francis, in
turn, ruled the tribe. The Indians became tired of the tribal relationship and

became citizens. They sold most of their lands about the Silver Creek church and purchased land northwest of Hartford near Rush Lake, Allegan County, Michigan. Each Indian family received a portion of land in its own name. Although citizens, the Pokagon band kept up some of their tribal formalities, such as electing a nominal chief. This honor for the most part was bestowed upon one of the youngest of the Pokagon children, Simon.

### Simon Pokagon

There are some differences in the statements about the time and place of Pokagon's birth. Some say he was born in 1825; other records would have it in 1830. Some say he was born at the old Pokagon village; others say he was born at the present village Pokagon where the family had gone to make maple syrup at a great maple camp located there. It is reasonably safe to say that he was born at the village of Pokagon in 1830.

Simon spent his childhood days at the old Pokagon village

*Courtesy of Northern Indiana Historical Society*

six miles northwest of South Bend. During this time he made many acquaintances with young white boys who remembered him in later years and who would relate pleasant experiences of their boyhood days together. At the early age of eight he moved with his family to the Long Lake neighborhood. When he was eleven his father died. Then he had years of college experience — four or five at Notre Dame, one at Oberlin and two at Twinsburg, Ohio. Some say his family wanted him to be a priest, but his inclination was not that way.

From his semi-autobiography, the Queen of the Woods, he tells us that he met his future wife, Lonidaw Sinagaw, while on a summer's trip to Black River in company with his mother and his friend, Joseph Bertrand, Jr. After a brief but serious courtship of one year, he left college to get married. He and his beautiful bride established a happy home. While he was always temperate himself, the curse of drink fell upon their home. The wife of his youth died in 1871 at the age of thirty-five. He had four children, Cecilia, William, Charles, and Jerome. He sent them to Haskel Institute for training. He did all he could to give them good training by himself. He was married a second time to a woman named Victoria. She outlived Simon, whose death occurred January 28, 1899.

Simon Pokagon lived an eventful life. It extended over most of the nineteenth century, during which time he saw the country pass from the ownership of the red man to the possession of the white man. He passed from a civilization that was most primitive to one of the most modern. He himself accepted much of this change with a genial spirit, though he must have suffered much. For years he endeavored to get the government to pay his people the money agreed upon for the sale of their lands. Although it was only three cents per acre, many unprincipled white men wanted to beat the Indian out of that. He did secure the payment of this money just a few years before his death. He himself received very little of this for the youngest baby of his tribe received as much in the division as he did.

During his entire life he made a bold fight against liquor. He had seen the awful effect of it upon his people and upon his own family. He was ever alert to stir up the people against this evil and was often called upon to make temperance addresses.

The great event of his life was when he was called to Chicago to take part in the World's Fair of 1893. Here he met some of his boyhood friends who had become wealthy men of Chicago. He was honored greatly and in turn performed a formal ceremony which had with it a touch of irony, in that he presented to the mayor of Chicago a deed for the land on which Chicago was built, a deed for the land the Pokagons once owned. Although the United States purchased this land at a price ridiculously small, for which payment was withheld for so many years, now since his people had recently received this money, Pokagon, as a great chief, presented to the white people a formal deed for it all. This was done on Chicago Day when Simon Pokagon was the guest of honor.

After he returned to his humble home in Michigan he received word from the Hon. Carter Harrison, mayor of Chicago, inviting him to come for another meeting to demonstrate the achievements of the Indian. Simon Pokagon went to Chicago to confer with his new friend. But as he arrived in the city the first thing he heard was that Mayor Harrison had been struck down by an assassin. Pokagon did not have the means himself to present what he would have desired. It is a wonder that some of his millionaire friends did not provide the money for this meeting and also contribute something to make the last days of their boyhood friend more comfortable.

The most of his life was spent in an humble dwelling near Rush Lake. For many years he took an active interest in the Rush Lake Catholic church, giving much help to the priests in their administrations. He loved music and for years was pianist at the church. He had a good library. One visitor tells about his surprise when he called at Pokagon's cabin and found Simon reading a Greek New Testament. He wrote much and went far and near to lecture, although he did not receive much for his services.

He became a fast friend of Charles Engle, editor and publisher at Hartford, Michigan. Mr. Engle encouraged Pokagon to write more. Mr. Pokagon did undertake to write a semi-autobiography in the form of an Indian romance. Mr. Engle proposed to finance its publication while the author looked forward to making lecture tours to advertise the new book. But even before it was printed Simon Pokagon was called to the Great Beyond to rest with his fathers. The book, however, was published under the name of Ogi-maw-kwe Mit-i-gwa-ki, or "The Queen of the Woods."

Much of this story is true, though there are some imaginary incidents and much poetic imagery. To encourage the reader of this history to read the whole of the excellent Indian story by Simon Pokagon and to add to the information about the Indian's ability to write, the following brief survey of the story is given.

Pokagon returned in the spring from college. He felt the Indian's urge to get back to nature. With his mother and one of the Bertrand boys, he went to the woods of the north for an outing. Across the stream from where he encamped, he saw a maiden with raven tresses and attractive ways. She had the power to mimic and attract to her all kinds of birds. With her at all times was a snow-white deer. He ventured to make her acquaintance and even to go to her home. To his surprise he learned that the maiden's mother and his own mother had been acquainted when they were girls, but each supposed the other was dead. The Indian maiden, whose name was Lonidaw, and her mother went with Pokagon to his own tent. Here the long-separated friends, their mothers, met and embraced each other lovingly. Lonidaw's mother told Pokagon's mother a sad story of her life.

She and her husband, Sinagaw, had lived at the Menominee village on Twin Lakes when the American soldiers came to take the Indians west. Her husband, Sinagaw, was one of the first to be captured. He saw that the soldiers intended to carry all Indians away. He sent word by a boy to his wife to tell her to flee. She did run away and hid in a hollow tree that night. There her baby girl was born. She named her Lonidaw. As soon as the mother was strong enough she took her baby and traveled far to the north, to the land of the Ottawa, where she met an old Ottawa trapper who took pity on them and helped them on in the world. Later the husband returned from the west, but he had taken to drink and soon died. The mother did all sorts of things to make a living for herself and daughter. Now here they were in the forest. The daughter would gather twigs and materials from the woods while the mother would make articles to sell to the white people.

The sad story of her life, only quickened Pokagon's love for Lonidaw. After another year in school he returned to claim her as his bride. They were wonderfully happy. Two children came to their home, a boy named Olandaw and a girl whom they named Hazeleye. They grew up in the forest, the joy of their parents. When the boy became old enough, the priest of that neighborhood encouraged the parents to send Olandaw to college that he might become a priest. Pokagon was favorable, but his wife, Lonidaw, was fearful lest something should happen to her son.

Olandaw did go to college and remained a few years. When he returned, his mother at once noticed that he had become addicted to drink. He gave her his promise that he would quit drinking but he could not. He went down in health and vice and soon died. Soon after Hazeleye was in a boat on the river when two drunken white men ran their boat into hers and threw her out into the stream. Her mother saw the tragedy from the shore and did all possible to rescue her daughter, but in vain. Hazeleye sank into a watery grave. The mother was brought ashore just as Pokagon arrived from the hunt and tried to revive and encourage her. But he could not. His darling Lonidaw, after incoherent talk, during which she made Pokagon promise that he would spend his life fighting drink, went on to the Spirit World to meet her daughter. Sad indeed were the funeral services for Lonidaw and Hazeleye. Here the author rises to his best in the pathos in which he expresses his loss and grief.

The remainder of the semi-autobiography and romance is largely devoted to the awful evil of drink and in appeals to the white men to save themselves and help save their red brethren from this great curse. The book has had a wide sale and is much liked by all who read it.

Little more can be said here about the last chief of the Pokagons and the last noted chief of the Potawatomi Indians. After his death some of his Chicago friends proposed to bury Simon Pokagon in Graceland Cemetery, Chicago, where some of his wealthy friends were buried. But very fittingly he had said that when he died he wanted to be buried in the land where he had lived. So he was buried back of the Rush Lake church beside the wife of his youth. A monument had been erected to her on which were these words: "Angeline, wife of Simon Pokagon, died December 1, 1871, aged 35." The last chief of the Potawatomi Indians has no stone for his grave, but this is just as he would have it.

*Left* — Long Lake Catholic Church near Dowagiac, Michigan, under which Leopold Pokagon and wife are buried.
*Right* — Jewett Pokagon and wife. He is a grandson of Simon Pokagon.

His descendants are with us today. They live in various places in southern Michigan, near Rush Lake and some of them near Long Lake. The accompanying picture is of Jewett Pokagon and his wife Susie Alexis. Jewett is a son of William Pokagon, a grandson of Simon Pokagon, and a great-grandson of the great chief, Leopold Pokagon.

While no great monument perpetuates the memory of Leopold and Simon Pokagon, and while few people know anything about the history of these great representatives of their race, their name has become familiar because of Pokagon State Park in Steuben County, Indiana. This park covers more than a thousand acres, and is a delightful place for the white man to take his rest and pleasure. It has some beautiful scenery that would remind you of the days when the red men hunted over this park as well as other lands that they owned. On Lake James has been erected a large hotel known as Potawatomi Inn. The park and the inn are monuments to the Pokagons and to the Potawatomi tribe who once owned this great empire.

**Courtesy of Potawatomi Inn**

# Bibliography

Indian Affairs — Treaties, Charles Kappler.

American Ethnology, 1896-97, H. W. Powell.

Handbook of American Indians, F. W. Hodge.

The Northwest and Chicago, Rufus Blanchard.

The Epic of Chicago, Henry R. Hamilton.

Checagou, Milo M. Quaife.

Western Annals, James Perkins.

Indian Tribes of North America, McKenny and Hall.

Indian Tribes of North America, Samuel Drake.

Harrison's Letters and Message, Edited by Logan Esary.

Indians and Indianans, J. P. Dunn.

True Indian Stories, J. P. Dunn.

Waubun, Early Days of the Northwest, Mrs. J. H. Kinzie.

Baptist Indian Missions, Isaac McCoy.

When Wilderness Was King, Randall Parrish.

Land of the Potawatomi, Elmore Barce.

The Potawatomi Indians, G. E. Lindquist.

Removal of the Potawatomi Indians, Daniel McDonald.

The Last of a Great Indian Tribe, Eaton G. Osman.

The Forest Potawatomi, Huron H. Smith.

The Mascoutens or Prairie Potawatomi, Alanson Skinner.

History of the Wabash Valley, Benj. F. Stuart.

Indian Reservations in Kansas, Anna Heloise Abel.

The Pokagons, Cecilia Bain Bueckner.

The Queen of the Woods, Simon Pokagon.

Made in United States
Troutdale, OR
11/13/2024

24726882R00051